PRAISE FOR ABUNDANT SOUL ABUNDANT LIFE

Ghary Won has done something quite extraordinary here. He has found an approach to sharing the great wisdoms of the world in a way that makes them totally accessible, completely understandable, and immediately applicable in everyday life. Seldom have I seen so much helpful information in one place. There's wonderful value between the covers of this book. Don't miss it.
Neale Donald Walsch, New York Times Bestselling Author of the *Conversations with God* Series

An extraordinarily penetrating and heart-centered approach to building a life of integrity and service. If you are looking for an impeccable guide to succeed as your authentic self, look no further. Learn from a true visionary how to follow your passion and vision. Ghary Won brings it all together in his unique inspiring way. The planet is a better place for this deep wisdom shared!
Alan Cohen, Author of the Award-Winning *A Deep Breath of Life*

Ghary is such a kind soul that everyone immediately relates to on a personal level, and he speaks with understanding and great wisdom that so many of us need today in order to live more vibrantly true to ourselves with flowing abundance, happiness, and love.
Ken Honda, International Bestselling Author of *Happy Money* and *True Wealth*

Copyright © 2024 by Ghary David Won

All rights reserved. No part of this book may be reproduced or transmitted in any form or by any means, electronic or mechanical, including photocopying, recording, or by any information storage or retrieval system without prior written permission from the author or their representatives.

This book is to be regarded as a reference source and is not intended to replace professional medical advice or prescribe the use of any technique as a form of treatment for physical, emotional, or medical problems without the advice of your physician. The author and the publisher disclaim any liability arising directly or indirectly from the use of this book.

Library of Congress Control Number 2024913983

Hardcover Edition 979-8-9910699-5-3
Paperback Edition 979-8-9910699-0-8
eBook Edition 979-8-9910699-3-9
Audiobook Edition 979-8-9910699-4-6

10 9 8 7 6 5 4 3 2 1 1st edition, October 2024

Printed in the United States of America
Published by Living and Dying Media Group
www.ladmg.com

ABUNDANT SOUL
ABUNDANT LIFE
THE ART OF LIVING YOU

GHARY DAVID WON

www.gharydavidwon

To Mom

*Who told me I'm a good writer,
even after I failed sophomore English.*

CONTENTS

Acknowledgments	ix
Foreword	xi
1. Fundamental Truths	1
2. The Human Development Cycle	27
3. Love Is All There Is	49
4. Following Your Passion	67
5. Loss, Death And Separation	85
6. Vibrational Reality	105
7. The Power of Gratitude And Worthiness	119
8. Money	139
9. Manifestation And Self-Sabotage	161
10. Authenticity	187
11. Joy, Happiness And Bliss	203
12. The Art Of Living You	221
Epilogue	239
Special Message from the Author	241
Bibliography	247
About the Author	249

ACKNOWLEDGMENTS

It is impossible to acknowledge all the wonderful people that I am grateful for without inadvertently leaving someone out. So just know I am grateful for you in my life and your faith in me. You know who you are.

However, during one of the most challenging times in my life while being homeless, I'd be remiss if I didn't personally acknowledge Thalya DeMott, Gerald deHeer, Donna Ruffin, and Bob Low, for all their help in keeping the tiny light lit at the end of the dark tunnel. They helped me find my way out and continuously reminded me that there would eventually be a tomorrow.

To my wonderful editor, Jami Lynn Sands, who as a long-time editor working with author Neale Donald Walsch, helped me to raise my confidence as a writer with her guidance on my manuscript.

To all the remarkable people who've made their own mark in the world because they had the courage to take the leap. Comedian, actor, songwriter and talk show host, Steve Allen, was the first person to recognize my ability to interview people and encouraged me to make it a part of my life.

To author Neale Donald Walsch, whose life and personal words of inspiration motivated me to finally get this into book form.

To Ken Honda, who gives so much of himself to make other people's lives better, including mine.

And to Alan Cohen, someone I've come to admire for his inspiring and loving approach to helping others in this world.

With Love and gratitude,
Ghary David Won

FOREWORD

As this is a book that offers incredible guidance on various topics that contribute to a happier life with more abundance, gratitude, self-worth, and peace, Ghary's insightful words inspired me to share my own thoughts on how to choose a path in life that leads to the greatest happiness and fulfillment.

If you are looking for direction in your life, it's essential to be more aware of your life purpose and recognize the overarching theme that stretches across your whole life. Many people these days are probably wondering about whether the work or lifestyle they live now is in fact the right choice or not, and whether what you're doing from day to day is contributing something positive to your life. I'm sure most of us actually feel a bit lost. How many of us could say honestly and confidently that the work you do now is in fact the reason you were born? The more common story is that we end up doing work that we fell into by luck or coincidence ten, sometimes twenty or thirty years ago. Even if many people change jobs a few times along the way, the general feeling is the same.

When presented with a choice to go in one direction or another, knowing the theme that strings your life together will actually make the answer much more clear. Knowing who you are and what you love actually lights up the path towards your greatest happiness, so you no longer feel lost and without purpose.

If you're reading this now, of course I have no way of knowing how old you are, but if you're in your 30's, let's say you have at least 30 or 35 more years of healthy life ahead of you. Knowing that many people encounter illness in their mid-sixties, that means if you're in your 50's you may only have 10 or 15 healthy and active years of life remaining. I'm not trying to scare you, but I'm just encouraging you to think practically about how you truly wish to spend the time left you have in this life.

What theme will you make your life about in these last few decades? Depending on who you are, the answer might be education, nutrition, health, or even business or psychology. What do you want to dedicate the rest of your life to exploring in greater detail or place near the center of your life as a driving force you follow with curiosity? Please think about what that answer is for you.

If you've picked up this book, it's highly likely you're interested in how to live with more authenticity, education, making life an expression of your true self, or perhaps even relationships. What feels to you like such an essential element of your life that you couldn't live without it? If someone told you you're not allowed to look at, touch, or interact with that one particular thing for the rest of your entire life, what is the thing that would be unbearable for you to be without?

For me, I would feel that way if someone told me I'm not allowed to read another book for the rest of my entire life. I don't think I could take it. But if someone said I wasn't allowed to play golf for the rest of my life, I might shrug and say that's okay. It wouldn't bother me at all because it just happens that I don't have the hobby of playing golf in the first place and it's just not an important part of my life.

Maybe in your case, you wouldn't bat an eyelash if someone told you that you're not allowed to go fishing ever again, but for another person it would feel devastating. Each of us will have a completely different answer because the important theme in our life is unique and different from everyone else. Maybe you love studying, yoga, or exercise. Any of these things and much more could be a huge theme in your life. The theme of your life is something that fills you with curiosity and excitement.

That being said, the theme of your life doesn't necessarily need to equal what you do for work. If you do yoga as a hobby for many years, it could be incredibly important to you, but that doesn't mean you need to do work in the field of yoga. In an act of synchronicity, you could meet someone at a yoga class who you hit it off with and you decide to start a business with that person completely unrelated to yoga. The passion and interest in yoga that drove you to attend those classes is one element that created the synchronicity that showed up to change your life. Things like this happen every day.

The theme of your life will be something so important to you that you would gladly spend the rest of your life diving into as deeply as possible. It's okay if it's simply a hobby you're very passionate about because who knows what kind of exciting doors will open by the simple act of you following your passion and dreams. Finding the theme of your life can dramatically shift your life up to a totally different dimension. So please follow your curiosity and continue to search for the answer that is meaningful to you.

Pursuing the things that make you feel curious, the things you love, and the things that bring you joy and excitement - this will absolutely connect you to synchronistic opportunities, mentors, meetings, and encounters that change your life. You love those things for a reason, and it's part of your destiny and lights up your path to happiness.

I wish you luck finding the answer for yourself, and I know the chapters ahead will help show you the way.

Ken Honda
International Bestselling Author
Happy Money and *True Wealth* books

CHAPTER ONE
FUNDAMENTAL TRUTHS

Why is it that some people are, or become, wealthy and others don't? What is the common thread between people who are wealthy and ruthless and those who are just as rich, but guided by generosity and kindness? And why does it seem that some people appear to breeze through life and others struggle? My fascination with this enigma led me on a long, long journey to discover certain truths. For the most part, I seemed to have chosen for myself the road less traveled, often taking detours along the way and usually stopping at most of the roadside distractions. I struggled, often feeling like I was resisting all the things that tiny voice inside was telling me. Not that I've regretted it mind you, because the hard-earned insights have awakened me to what is truly real in bringing abundance into my life. I have learned to see things in a different way, which has led to more peace and happiness in my life. I see the genius of all that is available to us that we can choose to experience or ignore completely on this amazing journey.

It's important that we realize that we live in this wonderful, but illusionary world, not to simply ride the highs and lows of life, but to realize that we are here to create, manifest, and express the greatest version of ourselves in the world. Let us begin by discussing some of the fundamental truths for a better understanding. The illusion is that our experience here in this physical world is what we call "real," that we are separate human beings, and that our main purpose is to acquire things, with the primary focus on the accumulation of money.

To create this separation, we exist through our egos, which helps us interpret the confusing contrasts in our world. It primarily uses external measures to help us determine our self-worth, how we should live, what we should own, and how well we are doing in comparison to our neighbor. So, our lives become more about competing, rather than about self-discovery. The opposite of this is to find purpose

ABUNDANT SOUL ABUNDANT LIFE

in our lives, where we measure ourselves internally, and realize that true abundance is about self-love and sharing that love with others. It's about living a happy and joyous life of authenticity with as much abundance as we wish to have. While monetary wealth is certainly one aspect of that abundance, it is not our greatest nor only asset.

Given that none of us will be able to keep any of the things we've acquired here when we leave this world, life is about the experiential nature of our emotions, feelings, and interactions with each other. Specifically, our task is to experience and express Love in all its variety of shades and hues. Money is one such color of Love, as is happiness. We discover the fullness of this life, by exploring, making mistakes, creating the most important things in our life, and having as much fun as we possibly can. The expression of Love is what our passion in life is, but it is our experience with Love that makes it all happen.

The goal here is to heal through our understanding of abundance, our–relationship with money, and how to create it. That happens by realizing this illusionary dimension was created for our benefit, not as a way to punish us. We will study the importance of living an authentic purpose-driven life, the deeper meaning of gratitude, and how our self-worth directly influences our level of abundance. This will lead us to find happiness, as well as how to address and deal with death and loss. You will learn why we face extremes such as fear and love, grief and happiness, wealth and poverty, life and death, and other seemingly opposing forces. Ultimately, we are here to support you on your journey by helping you to appreciate the contrasts of life so you can use them to transcend and discover that there is more to discover than we previously knew.

Our focus is not on relationships, except for the one between you and yourself and your relationship with Source God. That internal relationship is meant to help us thrive as abundant human beings, once we understand how to appreciate the differences of others and figure out where we fit in. The key to our success is all about helping others discover their self-worth and supporting them on their path of deciding what their purpose here is. When we do so graciously, we get everything we desire. In the end it's up to each of us to decide how we choose to live, and if and how we choose to contribute to the well-being of others. The option is always there to do nothing. We heal and awaken that abundant part of us when we get to a space where we feel worthy enough to be loved and to share that love with others and help them find their way. At that point, the abundance of the world arrives, knocking at our door, and asking to come in.

To be clear, there is only one reason why we're here and that is to experience and express Love to its fullest. By this expression of Love, and living a passion-driven authentic life, the abundance that we seek comes to us by helping others do the same.

We come from a place of complete Love to a place of artificial reality which we believe to be true. This artificial reality provides a stage or place to interact with one another. This is the place where we experience a separated identity from the God Source, known as the ego, to see others and ourselves in a different light. Here we decide how we want to act and appear to one another and how we fit into it all. This is crucial when it comes to our happiness and creating lifelong abundance in multiple areas of our lives.

Whatever beliefs you have acquired over your lifetime, I ask that you consider being open to viewing your life from a different perspective. There might be something that upsets you initially, but I urge you to keep reading. The fact that you found this book probably means you're ready.

Does God exist? Yes, of course, but not as an old man with a beard who judges us and rules over us. Rather, God is an energy of unconditional pure LOVE, as is everything else in the entire universe, that includes happiness and abundance. There are infinite "realities" all vibrating at varying speeds that allow each of us to experience that individualized part of God's energy. At the same time, each of us is this individual energy that makes up the limitless God force of Love.

In what feels like a separation between ourselves and others in this world, imagine that we are all actors performing in our own stage play where the theme is all about Love. However, we control the plot, with our script being continuously written through the moment-to-moment decisions and actions we make every day by who we wish to be and how we wish to live. More specifically, who we choose to outwardly express to others what our passion is in life. Hence, while there is a common theme to understand the energy of Love, there are an infinite number of ways of living it. As a caregiver, entrepreneur, artist, activist - the list is endless.

We must always remind ourselves that we ultimately can decide what we want our journey to look like.

"There is only one common destination we all seek in understanding the true essence of Love, but an infinite number of pathways to arrive there."

Perhaps we choose a straight road where our life is simple - or maybe one that is filled with a series of detours on rocky roads. Because we have free will, our script is unique from anyone else's and different with each trip we make here. What is common though, is that the ultimate destination for all of us is to experience and express Love. First to figure out what Love truly means to us. Then to love ourselves, love others, and love what we choose to do. We then use that to outwardly express the Love we have inside of us to help others discover their way.

While we exist in pure unconditional Love in Spirit before our arrival here, Love in this dimension is something that is found. It is not outside of ourselves, but rather inside. Herein lies all your answers and solutions. All our abundance is found within us, and it is not just about wealth and happiness. It also can include discovering a deep compassion for others, where you once had none. This illusionary world has us believe everything we seek is outside and beyond our control and many times beyond our reach.

Love is all there is. When we return to Source, we'll be asked two questions: "Did you experience and express Love to its fullest," and secondly, "Did you have fun while you were there?" Should we be surprised that so many songs poems, stories, and movies are written about love? Above all, Love is who we are because God is Love in its fullest expression described as "Unconditional" Love. For our visit here, it's important to remind ourselves that Love means more than that which is between two people. It can heal and raise us to great heights if we can discover a way to step into that state of being where we can know in our hearts that "I AM Love." If we're able to say this with true conviction, then we have come to a place where we have healed and awakened that part of us.

Source or Universal Consciousness or God's vibrational universal reality, by whatever name you choose, is meant to be a place of the never-ending experience and expression of Love in all its forms. Wealth, abundance, poverty, and lack are vibrational emotional variations of Love being expressed outwardly. In truth, we are Love incarnate and Love itself. We get to choose how we wish to BE in this physical world and how we go about making it possible.

In every moment of our lives, we either move toward or away from different things in our lives (such as money or happiness) through our emotions. Emotions regulate our vibrational energy, so positive feelings raise our vibrational energy making it easier to recognize and manifest the things we want. Consequently, negative feelings lower our energy, bringing other things we usually don't want into our lives.

> *"Since everyone and everything is energy,*
> *nothing ever 'dies',*
> *it just changes its form of vibrational energy."*

In this cosmology, life is not about being born into this world and then you die with a defined beginning and an end. Rather, it is an unbroken circle of "births," "deaths," and in between, filled with experiences and expressions of ourselves, all for the benefit of expanding the universe or God's consciousness that is in each one of us. Every single creature is a part of the omnipresent energy that we call God, and everything is expanding. In truth, it is impossible to separate ourselves from God's energy, but this wonderful illusionary stage of perceived gains and losses helps us to live out these individual experiences and contrasts. We can choose to feel alone as a separate person, or what we truly are as part of something greater—an integral undivided part of the universal God consciousness.

Everything has another side to it in this physical realm, but in the spiritual realm, there is none, as it does not exist. Therefore, we view everything here as separate. Both hot and cold water are at its basic essence, water - and our perception of the word "light" is measured in its intensity from a bright light or the absence of light or pure darkness. Life and death are merely two sides of the same coin having neither a beginning nor ending. The act of living and dying is meant to help us, regardless of how we view death. The concept of separateness is the key component of our lifetimes here. Without it, we would be unable to decide what type of life we wish to live. Yet at the same time, it's meant to keep us living small.

Thus, it is important to recognize how our perception of this division, including loss and death changes in our experience with it. It may inspire and empower us, as it opens up the opportunity to transcend normal societal beliefs and fears. Or it may disempower us for a good part of our lives if we allow it to, keeping us in fear and uncertainty. It is from these experiences that we form an idea of how we want to choose to live our life or as some may view it, express ourselves during this lifetime.

As soon as we're born into this world, we quickly become aware of the idea of being separate from each other, when as an infant, the umbilical cord is cut and we are no longer part of our birth mother. Herein begins our individualized identity or ego that assists us during this journey.

It is also important to understand the law of opposites that author, Neale Donald Walsch, covers so well in his Conversations with God (CWG) material. From my point of view, I also see this as being similar to the idea of the Chinese Yin and Yang where everything *is* and is neither positive nor negative. We spend our entire existence here making judgments of the differences between one another. It's no wonder that we spend a great deal of time disagreeing or fighting with others who are different in some way, whether it's because they look different than us, their social economic status, or have different beliefs, many of which we learned growing up or acquired through watching the news of our choice. Surprisingly, these are the comparisons that help us figure out who we are, what our passion is in this lifetime, and how we want to express ourselves to the world. The idea is to see our differences as something to value. The gift I ultimately give to others becomes the gift I give to myself. These answers don't come from just one important master or teacher, but from everyone we've crossed paths with. Let us always be mindful that an insight can come from many people and many incidences.

> *"The gift I ultimately give to others becomes the gift I give to myself."*

If our experiences cause us to have a negative response, we can choose to express that in two ways: Either by deciding to do something completely the opposite in our response or doing the same by carrying that same negative energy into our family to our kids and possibly to their kids.

The law of opposites will bring that which we resist to experience. Once we've experienced it and have come to a new understanding, it no longer becomes an issue. Just realize that coming to a new understanding might take a while or may never come if living in the ego.

> *"When the opposite arrives at our door, invite it in.*
> *When you finally ask it to leave,*
> *you will have become a new person."*

Resisting all these things from the past does no good if we don't gain anything from it. For all of our experiences, we should use it positively and make it a part of us rather than trying to discard it. When it becomes fully part of us, we no longer have to worry about facing that challenge because we understand how to react to it. Often, change comes slowly when we see the same issue repeatedly in our lives. The more experience we have, the easier it will be to move past it with less anxiety until it becomes a non-issue.

Those we encounter throughout our lives, be it family or others, help to shape our views, our fears, what's safe and what's not, who we can trust and who we can't trust, who we admire and who we dislike. They can be our parents, siblings, caretakers, and friends, and though difficult to accept, even our enemies or abusers are here because of an agreement we made with this group of souls that comprise our "soul family." The single-intention of these contrasting interactions with these souls is to again, provide a pathway to understand Love and receive the gift that we can share with others for their journey.

This will be one of the most difficult things to understand and accept because, for some, their past experiences were so unbearable, that all that is possible is to "get over the past and move on." This is certainly understandable. There are so many atrocities that we do to each other that when viewed from seeing ourselves as separate from each other, it's hard to comprehend. If you are one such person, all I ask is you consider a different way of observing those situations. This ultimately offers us reasoning and empowerment for the terrible experiences we've suffered. Our move from a place of being the victim to one of becoming a Source of positive energy to those who've experienced similar tragedies is what can manifest if we choose to open our hearts to this different understanding.

We all have a choice in deciding how we allow things to affect us. It might be a hatred for someone or a shame we've held that keeps us from moving on because we still have a heavy heart at the memory of any part of that past. Or we can view it as a way of empowering ourselves and using the traumatic experience for good by helping someone else who is still living in fear and despair.

For some of us, there are reasons why we were bullied in school or had parents who either abandoned us or suffered from alcohol abuse, making it a challenge growing up. Many experiences we have originate from family and friends directly doing something to us - or because we misunderstood and/or misinterpreted something quite innocent. Whatever the way, it can affect us for a lifetime if we choose to continue to hold onto it. However, it is the goal of this journey to expand our understanding of ourselves and the world around us.

In my personal experience, it took me years to realize I had misinterpreted something my father said in passing when I was around 5 years old. I remember standing next to Dad during one of our Christmas parties with family and friends. As was the case with Dad's friends, it was common that they would banter with each other. On this occasion, standing in the living room of our lovely suburban home with the station wagon in the garage, friends and family would congratulate him on his successes, even though looking back I'd say we were a middle-class family of four at that time. Dad worked hard to live the American dream. His father/my grandfather was a vegetable farmer, and all his siblings were teachers. Growing up Chinese in Hawaii during those days meant you were either a merchant, a farmer, or in education. My father chose to move from a teacher to the world of business in insurance and later as a real estate appraiser and developer.

In the true fashion of an Asian father, he denied these signs of success and tried to downplay how well he had been doing for our family. In my little 5-year-old mind, I mistook his modesty for being embarrassed about success. From that moment on, I spent years wanting to "stay under the radar" and be like every other kid in public school. I saw money as something that embarrassed me.

While that experience might not seem to be very significant, it formed a basis for how I felt about myself. It affected how I interacted with others and how I let others treat me. What seemed like something so small and insignificant based on one innocent experience, lay dormant and hidden within me for decades. The road to healing our abundance is often hidden in something so inconsequential that it takes us years to uncover it for healing to take place. It was not just about how I viewed money but also being afraid to excel at anything. Being the center of attention made me believe ridicule was sure to follow. It would be years before I realized this was a false assumption.

This misunderstanding created a situation whereby I wanted to live "hidden," creating a difficult relationship between me and money. It became such an issue that it left me homeless for about ten months as an adult. The blessing was that it all contributed to who I am today. I now see how the contrast of my past has enabled me to understand and be more compassionate toward others facing similar challenges. For now you must understand that many things we deem as negative in our lives, end up being wonderful gifts if we're able to transcend and use the experience to ultimately share the full experience with others.

The ultimate expression of Love, of course, is how we choose to live our lives. One driven by passion and authenticity, or another by fear. While the former is certainly preferable for many of us, remember that some of us choose to experience fear either for our benefit or for the benefit of others we meet. Regardless of which way a person chooses to live during this lifetime, I say again that our only purpose is to experience Love to its fullest. First, by experiencing and understanding self-love and where to find it, we can heal past wounds. Then we go on to Love others through the expression of what we discover to be our gift to the world. Some may choose not to seek that path at all, which is their choice.

Like an infinite number of things in this physical realm, we are provided with a way for us to see, feel, and have an emotional reaction to an experience we may or may not believe we deserve to have. But if everything is Love, it's important to see all these things as gifts to help us, hard that it may be for some to hear. Simply put, both positive and negative emotions serve to help us. It is through contrast that we have the opportunity to decide who we are and how we want to live our lives as human beings living in this physical experience.

Therefore, the challenges we faced growing up that we characterize as negative, can be used to empower us if we so choose that expression. Understand that all experiences we have are the result of either someone doing something to us or what we do to ourselves. It may be our mother or father, siblings, friends, or enemies. Or it could be someone else completely on the other side of the world that makes us upset or afraid. Every experience is an opportunity for us to decide how we want to recreate ourselves in the grandest and most incredible vision of who we wish to express. In other words, to follow our passion for what we want to do in this lifetime that either brings joy to our heart each day or presents us with a major challenge - both of which seek to open our hearts. It is the presence of Love that allows us to see our "enemies" as having the same goals in mind. The purpose is to strengthen us, to give us more courage, to assist us in valuing ourselves more, to help us understand compassion, and to have us connect with the Love that always exists within us.

Many of us know that some of the most challenging times in our lives are an opportunity that allows us to grow significantly once we're able to emerge from the darkness of our fears and sorrow into a place of understanding.

Unexpected life challenges offer us the ability to transcend them and have an "aha! moment" of clarity. At the time when we're going through it, questions like "Why did this happen to me?" or "What can I do to stop feeling this way?" become foremost in our everyday consciousness. In reality, the physical realm is all about contrasting experiences for us to decide how we would like to spend our time here expressing that which we are.

Perhaps you are wondering why someone would agree to experience the grief of losing loved ones. Or be challenged with an addiction leading to a marriage break up or losing everything and ending up homeless. While it may seem to be unbearable at the time, the severity of the experience is what makes us stronger if we choose to crawl through the darkness to emerge on the other side. It allows us to take the things we experience, learn from them, and use them to eventually help others. Our greatest fears assist us in figuring out what our passions are.

Some experiences are so painful and difficult that we may ask, "Why, God?" It is said that God doesn't give us anything we can't handle. For many, the challenge of loss and the resulting separation is the most difficult. But now in this physical realm, this idea of separation is for our benefit. This can be something extreme involving the death of someone we love or as simple, but scary, as us losing our wallet or purse with all our ID and credit cards inside. One appeared to be devastating, the other, more than a nuisance. Both can make us react emotionally, although at different intensities. Yet it's important to remember these experiences are opportunities to embrace anger, despair, and sorrow, or love and happiness. I'm not saying it's wrong to experience grief. This is a natural human experience. But it's what we choose to do after that when we're able to emerge from the darkness of sorrow and grief and realize all that exists in this universe is Love. It's meant to open our hearts to so much Love that at some point, we have this incredible feeling and compulsion to share this Love with others. Many people refer to this as "living your passion," but it could be more accurately described as, "Love expressed to its fullest measure."

Keep in mind that some may choose to experience poverty to understand and ultimately express compassion or generosity in themselves and subsequently to others. While others may intentionally make the journey to experience loss and the lessons of separation through multiple deaths of the people closest to them, discovering the strength and self-confidence within themselves. A few may make this trip by transitioning (dying) early as a child or infant so that the people "left behind" have their own experience with the loss that has been presented to them. Experiences such as these have us questioning our reality and purpose in life. Herein begins the journey of the soul where we question what we're here to do.

Some Native American tribes have a ritual called the Vision Quest where the young brave would venture out alone on a journey to discover their place in the world and return to the tribe to assume their role in that community. Dr. Wayne Dyer used to call this, "dying while alive" whereby the ego dies, only to be reborn to a life driven by our desire to express. I see so many similarities between the Vision Quest to the Hero's Journey made famous by Joseph Campbell. Through his studies of mythology, he believed everyone, at some time in their life would make this Hero's Journey. This is where the Hero sets off on a glorious quest, and ultimately slays a metaphorical dragon within themselves to discover who they are. The dragon, akin to having an epiphany or an "Aha! moment," is meant to represent the dying of the ego self. It is our rebirth to knowing what we passionately wish to share with others as in the Vision Quest.

In both cases, whether we're talking about the demise of the child or ego within all of us or the hero before their "Aha! moment," our focus before the metamorphosis is on ourselves. But after the transformation, it moves to an outward expression of our experience with others. We do that by sharing our passion with others who care to accept it, to inspire them to do the same on their journey. We all have free will, so it's safe to say that not everyone will choose this path and not every soul will make the journey.

So, the important question to ask is, "Then why not create an incredible life full of abundance for ourselves?"

To live an incredible life in abundance is not necessarily being famous where you touch millions of people and make a lot of money. Nor does it mean being the greatest basketball star or changing the world in your job or being one of the richest people in the world.

Your life could also be described as incredible as a mother or father, by being someone that helps just one other person come to understand the true meaning of Unconditional Love and that person goes on to do the same with another human soul. Or it could be a factory worker whose hard work and tenacity inspire their children. So, whatever you choose to do, do it to the best of your ability. There are many ways to live incredibly so when you're ready to return to Source, you'll be prepared to answer whether you fully experienced and expressed Love.

CHAPTER ONE QUESTIONS

Take a few minutes to consider each question before answering in your journal. Write as much as you're inspired to. Review later after reading the entire book to see if your answers have changed in any significant way.

- What kinds of positive and negative emotions do you experience on a day-to-day basis? Would you say it's taking you away or toward what you wish for in life?
- What are your beliefs about death?
- Name three people in your life who are not considered financial or spiritual gurus who have been extremely influential (either positive or negative) in your development. What impact did each have on you?
- What is one possible gift that someone you consider as your enemy, tormentor, or abuser has given you?

CHAPTER TWO
THE HUMAN DEVELOPMENT CYCLE

This wonderful adventure we've come here to experience can be broken down into stages as a roadmap to human development. If we were to use the metaphor that all the world's a stage, then we could also view it as multiple acts of our play.

In the opening scene, our soul moves from formless and pure Love to merge with our physical bodies brought to "life" in our mothers. It is at this point that the symbolic umbilical cord that serves to nourish us is cut, producing our first experience of being an individual. Although the connection with the unified field of the infinite is never disconnected, at this stage, we come to understand the concepts of "I and Other," "I am I," and "You are You."

Here is where the ego is born to allow us to have the experience of contrast in this world. We now find ourselves living in a place in which we feel we are no longer part of the whole and detached from the Unconditional Love of God's Source - although it never leaves us. In our former state of being Oneness, it is impossible to experience true separation and individualization, hence the reason for us wanting to be here is to experience the contrast and help expand the Universe. There are still some lingering feelings of desiring to be part of something; however, as we grow we get used to the idea of separation.

The second act or stage of development is the recognition of space and time, where we sense distance, space, and the idea of time in the context of a past, present, and future. A Course in Miracles suggests that time is merely a construct of the ego in this illusionary world to keep us in fear, believing we are separate from the immense power and Love of the God Consciousness. As individual beings, time keeps us constantly focused on the past and present. This belief has us thinking we exist in a linear reality of defined limits. Think about how you assess your progress at the end of the year or live by deadlines. The present is the only place in this physical reality where we can take action on our so-called future dreams. Most problematic is seeing that the life we wish for is somewhere in the future. In reality, there is only the present, so what we wish to have or be exists in the same space. All that is required is to step into BEING that which you already are. There is no place to go, no place to return from, there is no future to work towards. This is why manifestation is so difficult, which we shall examine in another chapter.

For the infant, time as we know it is only a concept at this early stage. Knowing we're late for school comes later. While time itself is an illusion in the physical world, it does offer us the benefit of helping us. Overcoming unpleasant issues from the past sheds some light on what might be holding us back in the present. It also enables us to understand and appreciate things like gratitude which leads to worthiness. We've all had situations where we've endured something unpleasant from the past and some we've picked up along the way, whereas now looking back we can be grateful for having passed through that. Within the context of contrast, time allows us to see how much we've accomplished. A more detailed discussion of time is an intricate one and will not be covered in this book. However, it is one of those things that are part of this illusionary world to ultimately help us or constrain us in our search for meaning and manifesting our desires.

In the third act, as we grow, so does our ego. We look to others to give us clues to our identity. Here is where we decide how to act; what we should do, and what we shouldn't do. How can I get others to like me and what is and what is not acceptable? It is a period where we discover that external achievements are important to our identity, believing the answer to success, Love, and happiness lies outside of us. So, we tell ourselves, "If only this will happen, I can feel good about myself." Living with this identity, we measure ourselves in comparison to others as to how much we own, what kind of job we have and do we have the respect of others, which are all external measures of our self-worth. It is being downright unauthentic and dishonest as to how we see ourselves, hiding behind this mask of the ego. Life becomes more about competing with everyone else as we use other measures that hold very little meaning to live in our truth.

With lingering memories of Source and being still part of the wholeness of the One and the Love from that, many of us will feel the awkwardness of being different than others with feelings of wanting to be accepted even at this very young age. The desire to fit in with others tends to be universal at this stage. Since Love and happiness are no longer a given, we begin to search for them outside of ourselves.

While we all had the same goal in common to be "accepted" and loved during our early years as we sorted out how to live and grow, there are many unique reasons why the overwhelming need to fit in arises. Alas, the very act of "needing" is an illusion because it implies we are not whole and not enough. The truth is we need nothing and are already complete. It is this world of separation that has us believe we lack in some way. A very common example was being bullied in school for being different, like being smart or not wearing the "right" clothes. It's helpful to realize–the kids who were doing the bullying were also trying to fit in and be accepted as well.

This process we all go through is the first hint of the discovery of our self-worth and is, for the most part, universal in our journey here. It created the contrast for us to be confident in our later decisions of what we wanted for ourselves, what we felt we deserved to receive, and what we wanted to share with others, which is essentially the ultimate goal of being Loved. But before that can occur, we move to a place where our ego grows to assume more of a responsibility in making decisions in our lives.

In that stage, the ego has matured and is given free rein to decide how we want to live, how we interact and relate to other people, and how to feel about ourselves. It has us believe that Love exists outside or is lacking in us, encouraging us to be forever searching for people and things to make us feel adequate and whole and loved. The ego convinces us that the true love we yearn to experience and express does not exist or is extremely rare, when in fact it is impossible to disconnect from the God Source of Unconditional Love. The ego forces us to create a mask or barrier to hide behind so that our true selves and true feelings aren't rejected. It convinces us that vulnerability is something to avoid at all costs, lest we be hurt by others. Rather than living authentically and being honest with ourselves, we portray a false image to others, hoping they will accept this alter ego identity, but we worry about the consequences of living this way.

While it's clear that relying on the ego is the way of struggle and hardship, the development of it has an important purpose as we grow up. It promotes the illusion of separateness and time so we're able to see things from a different perspective. And with that, it allows us to experience the contrast so we can decide how to express ourselves. More importantly, our egos serve to protect the true nature of our self at this age. It keeps us from knowing certain truths about ourselves and our reality that we can't handle, so lies are created to cope. The danger of living too much in our ego is that we begin to believe we as individuals are the source and power of all our answers, allowing fear to overwhelm us. Narcissistic people tend to be extreme examples of this, developing a misplaced view of their self-importance.

Living in ego, we make plans and figure out the exact and quickest route to take, knowing when we will arrive and going against that inner voice telling us otherwise. Life is never a straight road to our destination. There are always detours we can choose to make and roadside distractions along the way that enrich our experience. However, it is through the prism of the ego that we see these roadside pitstops, or anything other than what was originally planned, as going down the wrong road.

When we use our ego in the pursuit of our dream of who we wish to be in this lifetime, it is always about others and how we seek to impress or hurt them in one way or another to make us feel accepted or accomplished - what I'm owed or what I believe I deserve to be paid. It all comes from the perspective of external recognitions and measures of valuing ourselves.

As such, the challenge is to look closely at the plans we make, especially when we honestly believe they are made to help others. We fool ourselves into thinking what we're doing is for others when it's really to make us look good in another person's eyes, and succeed at being better. On closer inspection, we see that it is for the sole benefit of ourselves rather than others. I wonder if this is where the phrase, "feed the ego" came from. Because it arises out of seeking to impress others to get them to do something for us, it's always good to ask ourselves, "What is the real reason I am doing this?"

In contrast, when we live an authentic and passion-centered life, the reward comes from the internal satisfaction of what we do every day. And that includes loving ourselves, which can only originate from within us. When living through our authenticity, we are already receiving what we want on a moment-to-moment basis each day. We just have to remember to focus on others and their success and by doing so, everything we want shows up.

The ego, unfortunately, at this stage in life, is the place where dreams for a truly purposeful life go to die. Here again, rather than trying to impress people, a better way is to focus on expressing ourselves to others through the discovery and pursuit of our purpose during this lifetime. True abundance comes as a result of being honest with ourselves and that helps us discover ways to live out a life focused on a deep-seated passion. This is when we experience positive emotions that bring us happiness, contentment, and the manifestation of what we wish for. By living this way, it's not necessary to ask ourselves the question of whose benefit is it for, because we have already received our reward. Living this way is not a necessity but it makes it a whole lot easier.

> *"Rather than IMPRESSING others,*
> *work towards EXPRESSING yourself."*

So, the next step in our journey is a choice to either move to a place where we pursue this type of life or where we continue to live as an individual self. This is where we're using external cues and self-recognition rather than choosing selflessness. It is a choice we may find difficult to make, but it gets easier over time. I still catch myself occasionally comparing my progress to friends of mine, which gives me pause so I can stop and evaluate what I'm doing.

This is certainly not to say an ego-driven life is not about helping others, as it has just as much meaning as one driven by authenticity and passion. It's just that it's so damn hard and more of a struggle. Many ego-driven people certainly can live a lifetime being role models of what a good father is or through experiencing success. However, life tends to be more of a struggle and feel lonely at times because we keep looking for Love and happiness outside of us. Most people in this category may describe their lives as "hard" and "difficult." Uncomfortable feelings that maybe we've come here for a reason, are quieted by the ambitions of the ego. Sometimes it takes years for us to realize we're not happy and shouldn't have been following what made sense, but rather what makes our hearts flutter. We can be comforted by the fact that all that came before, prepares us for tomorrow.

It is not uncommon for all of us to experience this knowing that there's a greater purpose to our life and the false need for a bigger expression of ourselves. Depending on how uncomfortable it becomes or if we're able to break away from the lure of the ego, some of us will embark on a hero's journey of discovery to figure out how we fit into this world. This desire mirrors both the Native American Vision Quest ethos and Joseph Campbell's, The Hero's Journey metaphor.

The concept of both endeavors is about "dying while you're alive," as author Dr. Wayne Dyer would say. It is essentially that of the young brave, who is tasked to go out into the wilderness alone to discover what his place in the tribe is. He is alone but is accompanied by the spirits that help him through this journey, and when he returns, the child has "died" and the adult now takes their place in society.

Joseph Campbell's model of the Hero's Journey is similarly based on the individual's search for meaning and the subsequent "death" of a part of us. This happens through the challenges and eventual slaying of our inner metaphorical dragons that keep us from recognizing there is more to life than just us in the world. We no longer feel burdened by living a life that others want us to live. It is the conquering of an ego-centered life and giving in to that individualized focus. Rather, we're led to discover the true Love inside of ourselves so that we may venture off on a heroic purpose. This is where we live as authentically honest to who we are and satisfy that deep yearning we have inside us. While anyone can make this journey, some may choose not to do so during this lifetime and just remain living through their ego.

What precedes the hero setting off on their quest into the unknown is usually an uncomfortable sense that their life is going nowhere, as certain questions keep coming up. Why am I so unhappy? Is this all there is? What the ego taught us is that success is achieved by constantly trying to impress and being in competition with others. But that type of life based on seeking approval and emotional assurances from others no longer is important. Instead, the questions are, what is my real purpose for being here and how can I share myself with others to help them express their own gift? Much of this has to do with an expanded version of our self-worth, whether we're worthy enough to be Loved and express Love to others. The greater the extent we love ourselves, the more abundance we allow ourselves to experience.

During the next phase, the hero begins their adventure and is faced with various challenges, obstacles, and adversities that are meant to break through long-standing relationships they've had with their egos. While this journey may take months or years sometimes, its ultimate goal is to put aside our egos through self-love. All the hurt that others inflicted upon us and the subsequent wounds that followed are now seen as gifts. We see those people that helped us to experience contrast were in fact, catalysts for us so that we may decide how we wish to act from here on out.

The one beautiful thing about life that most of us fail to understand while we experience this stage play of our own making, is that every single person we come in contact with, in some form or another, helps to shape our view of things or how we now act. It gives us, as author Neale Donald Walsch says, "the opportunity to recreate ourselves in the grandest vision of who we are from that point forward." We move from feeling victimized as the result of someone else's will, or worse yet, what we inflicted upon ourselves, to one of positive empowerment essentially to love ourselves.

It is the turning point, the epiphany or "Aha!" moment of clarity to see and appreciate the wonderful symphony we all play together as we each play our part with our unique instrument in harmony. And many times, it's the challenging situations we had little faith in overcoming such as alcohol or drug addictions, being homeless or perhaps being abandoned as a child, that allow us to discover what role we want to play in our tribe - what Love we want to express to others. With that, the hero returns home from his journey to get to work and begin a new journey in a purpose-driven life.

Not everyone will make the journey down that road less traveled. Some will see it and make plans for it yet will never embark on their journey. Or they will give up and feel more comfortable staying where they are.

However, when we do make the journey or embark on our own vision quest, we can experience the inner transformation of not having to rely on our egos. There emerges a series of events that unfold:

- We see our achievements from our internal perspective, so our measure of success is based on internal accomplishments and satisfaction.
- We evaluate ourselves by looking inward so our identity and value comes from within, without a reliance on having others acknowledge us.
- We gain confidence and strength in what our role here is through seeing the success of others. The connection to a spiritual life becomes real and our goals are no longer self-oriented, but rather society inclusive driven.
- We come to realize that there are no needs and that we already had everything when we first arrived. The challenge is to remember we are part of the whole of the universe and to step into that power.
- We do this by relaxing into it, stopping trying to get there, and accepting that we already are because the future is an illusion. There is no place where we are trying to get to, knowing that we have already arrived. The sooner that happens, the sooner we manifest it into our lives. The journey is not

complete, however, until we find a way out of our comfort zone.

Authenticity now becomes the prime motivator. Important questions we ask ourselves are:

- Am I being honest with myself and how I express myself to others?
- How may I be of service in the expansion of God's consciousness, knowing that through my service, everything I want flows to me easily?

We now devote our time to expressing who we are and living our life of passion. And although the ego still exists, we suspend our reliance on it to protect us or impress others in order for us to move forward. Putting aside the ego opens us to reconnect with the power of Source and the present moment where all manifestation takes place.

This is not to say that all our past wounds are resolved, but life is now more about joy and happiness. This makes it easier to understand how these past experiences helped us, rather than hindered us, making the manifestation of our dreams possible. It is a time when we feel worthy and accept the Love coming to us so we can share the same with others freely and without conditions.

Regardless of how the change comes about, our perception of how we see ourselves and the outer world and what's important shifts. Achievement comes from internal success and our focus is on sharing our gifts with others to expand the universe, intent on expressing Who We Are or what we wish to share with others.

The ultimate benefit of living on purpose is that we shift to living authentically. If that resonates with you, you're either feeling the pains of discontentment or already on your own hero's journey. If that is the case, then live towards being authentic as best you can and embody the notion that you ARE Love.

I have said that authenticity is about being honest with ourselves in everything we do, in what we choose to do for a living, in how we treat other people and ourselves, accepting responsibility for our lives knowing every good and bad thing is here to provide a contrast so we can decide how we want to act going forward.

It's important to come to embrace all those very things we want to avoid or hate about ourselves. At that point, what we spent a lifetime fighting becomes yet a memory, but still very much part of Who We Are. I think this is why people who have experienced extreme challenges in their lives end up being the best teachers of that problem. This happens when they can emerge from the darkness of a bad situation to understand there are no demons or victims here. The greater the past burden, the better able to serve others with a similar problem. They move towards a more authentic self, an honesty that is now a true expression of their Love which people are attracted to.

*"The deeper the hurt,
the greater your ability to heal others
by the gift you've been blessed to have received."*

The process by which we become more authentic is to make peace with our ego and don't outright reject it. It has been there to help us understand and discover our authentic selves. All it knows is to protect us and if that means sabotaging ourselves, understand it for what it brings to us. Bless it and realize it's not bad. The ego is also necessary to understand what we don't want, by seeing the contrast and wishing to experience what we do want. Let go of fighting and let go of the outcome. Let go of the notion of destroying the ego just because it's the opposite of what we want. Instead, work with it and see it as a helpful partner in getting to where we want to go.

Use it to see how much Love we can experience from the passing of someone close to us by turning the sadness and despair around when we're ready to open up our hearts again. Instead, discover the joy and happiness inside us so we can now turn to assisting someone else. Who better to help a despondent couple who's lost their child than a parent that had faced such a loss themselves and to have emerged onto the other side to Love?

Authenticity also means to be open and willing to be vulnerable, knowing that others in the world are here to challenge us and help us, all from the perspective of Love. When we open ourselves up to showing who we are, there are fewer things that people can attack us for, removing the necessity to defend ourselves. Before reaching this state, we often ask ourselves, how much Love do I deserve in this world? In truth, when we become fully authentic, we ARE COMPLETE LOVE. At this stage, there are no more victims, there are no more tormentors, there are no more villains.

So, in a sense, we gain our power in the process. Authenticity is essentially being honest with ourselves and our feelings, especially for us men, who have a hard time being vulnerable in front of other people. Few people realize that vulnerability raises our influence on others as our power comes from our authenticity rather than by force - from ourselves internally rather than externally.

Some people who choose to live a ego-driven life may never reach authenticity even as they are dying, even though it's a time when there's little reason to still put on appearances or be embarrassed about something. They may need to be stripped away of this layer in the very last stage of their human development as they move back into Spirit and their soul opens its eyes to the fact that it's always been a part of the whole of God and the illusion of separateness is no more.

Whether we've chosen to live from the ego, one of higher purpose, or even just to make the trip here for the benefit of others, everyone will encounter the next stage of human development as we move towards transition and a return to Source. We are essentially leaving this existence in the opposite direction whence we came. Here is where we lose all perception of space, followed by time. There is little reason to care about our past and our future is all but certain. All of it becomes irrelevant on our deathbed.

The final stage is what many refer to as death, which is a return to Spirit or Source. Here, the ego dissipates, and the separation where everything as seen in the reference of "I" and "other" drops away. We only see ourselves and everything else as Source and all there is, is God.

CHAPTER TWO QUESTIONS

Take a few minutes to consider each question before answering in your journal. Write as much as you're inspired to. Review later after reading the entire book to see if your answers have changed in any significant way.

- How many detours or stops along the way have you experienced? Did it help or was it a waste of time? If a waste of time, explain why you believe that.
- Would you say you currently rely on your ego most of the time to interface with the world? How do you know? Remember that when you use others as a measure of your success or how well you're doing, then this is a sure sign you are still living through your ego.
- Would you say most of your life is about trying to impress others, or about expressing your true gifts to the world?
- Do you know how you fit into the world? Write a brief paragraph describing it.

CHAPTER THREE
LOVE IS ALL THERE IS

This is one of the most important chapters because if you understand the root principles of what is written here, they can be applied to anything you want to manifest in your life to be truly abundant. To understand the importance we place on Love, let me quote something from the very last episode of the 2011 American television series "Suits".

"From the day we're born we look for Love,
Because it is Love that nourishes our soul.
And when we're lucky enough to find it
Our lives are changed forever."

To be perfect, I would add the following:

*"Just remember that Love comes from inside each of us.
That is where our search begins.
Luckily, we won't have that far to go."*

The first chapter was all about our entire existence being that we are a part of God - or Source or Universal Consciousness, or whatever name you use. Since God is Love, then it follows that everything, everywhere is made up of Love - more specifically, Unconditional Love. In the physical realm, however, we experience a reality that is just an illusion where this artificial construct of division and separation has been created. This is specifically to help us discover ourselves while expanding the Universe, thereby making us believe we are apart from the energy of Love and happiness.

Being separated from one another, there are an unlimited number of choices on how we can interpret the meaning of our interactions with other people that we encounter. Filled with opposing sides to show us the contrast, love exists in relationship to fear. Everything has a corresponding opposing partner to allow us to experience both sides if we so choose to do so. It allows us to form an opinion and

ABUNDANT SOUL ABUNDANT LIFE

decide for ourselves how we want to live. Life is about contrast, such as hot and cold, loud and soft, being incredibly wealthy or living in extreme poverty, seeing the wonderful beauty of it all, or focusing on the ugliness and limitations. It's about living in constant joy and happiness, or opting instead to live in sadness and despair, or the proverbial glass half full or glass half empty. Why would anyone choose to live in poverty or in such an extremely challenging life? For the timeless soul, our existence is more than living lives where everything is easy and comfortable, strange as it may be.

In terms of the law of opposites, we are the ones who create our challenges so that we may experience them. We come to discover the opposite and by that process, choose one or the other. The result of this contrast may help us in changing how we see things, or it may reinforce it, resulting in becoming more certain in our view of something. Or it could flip it on its side to now take the opposing view. The total of all of this eventually allows us to decide how we want to act with others and how we want to express that outwardly. It follows then, that through our most challenging and often extreme experiences, we're able to come to understand and transform ourselves.

Remember, there is only one reason for our existence here and that is to experience Love and express that to others. How we choose to do that and by what means it takes to come to that understanding is up to us to decide. We could choose to be a wonderfully caring person that loses their entire family as a result of a drunk driver. Or spend a good portion of our life as a homeless person who meets someone one day that flips their life upside down. Love comes in all different shades and hues.

*"Label not thy enemy
for they may turn out to be our savior."*

The process of discovery is the process of remembering who we are so we can step into BEING that. Since the future is only an illusion within this physical realm, the challenge is overcoming the idea that what you desire is far away. It is actually a matter of stepping into that which you wish to be. Time creates that imaginary wall between us and what we imagine as "our future self that we yearn to be."

*"The journey to our future self is a long one,
until it no longer is."*

The "Aha! moment" of clarity for the Hero on its journey is the realization that the extremely difficult experience we had, now actually empowers us to be able to help someone else. Here is where we gain meaning and purpose to our existence if we choose to do so. This is the process by which we arrive at deciding what our passion in life is through choosing authenticity over ego, of living with our eyes open, or being stuck in a world of illusion. In other words, it is how we figure out what "Love expressed" means to each one of us. But the choice is still ours. Do we follow one guided by this passion that's been ignited within us or ignore it and stay behind the mask and barrier of the ego?

As I said earlier, the challenge of living in the latter is that we end up relying on things outside of us to give us validation, to make ourselves feel whole and loved. So negative encounters we have in our lives are viewed as unwelcome and often with disdain. "My parents are to blame for the way they treated me and my siblings and that's why I struggle now in life." In this space, we're also asking, "How do I measure up compared to Mr. or Ms. X?" We often see ourselves as less than whole and "not yet arrived" and worried about being called out as an imposter. Our success is usually determined by how much we earn or what brand of car we own, that is, after 84 months of payments to the bank of course.

Even in this passion-driven world, it's important to remind ourselves that it's not just the realization that we are all Love, but more importantly, that as Love, we have the power to create things, to help heal others, and to help others live their own passionate experience if they so choose. All of this occurs through us living a truly inspiring and authentic life. This is how we can be that shining star for others to live out their own true desires.

Remember that from the moment we're born, Unconditional Love is no longer a given, as now it's a choice. Instinctively, we know that Love nourishes our soul and when we're able to connect with it again, our lives change forever. But until we move towards living one that is passion-driven, our egos will always tell us there is nothing out there and that we live in a world of struggle to find Love and to keep it. As such, we spend a lot of time searching for it outside of us, working hard to keep it, and afraid we'll lose what precious little we have of it. It is the same way with money and everything else in our lives because we see it separated from us far into the "future," outside, often hard to obtain, and out of reach for many. It's important to remember that this discussion of the role of Love has all to do with whatever earthly desires we wish for, whether it be money, a nice car, a prestigious job or profession, a beautiful home, or whatever. All those expectations are perfectly fine as long as we don't use them as a measure of our self-worth or how well we're doing.

The path of discovery to understand how "Love is all there is," starts with looking inward and loving ourselves by realizing all of our past hurts are now growth opportunities. We must ask ourselves if we're worthy enough to be loved or have enough love inside ourselves. That is the prelude to being able to share that with others. Plus, knowing if our life is in line with our core beliefs and living as authentically as we can.

This is seen as the start of our move towards less reliance on the ego to protect us and as a way of seeing our lives in a completely different way. It's important to take the time to examine each of our past relationships that we experienced or failed to experience and how that affects us even today. It may be necessary to release any past bitterness or anger we had with them or still hold onto them and evaluate each incident in a way that's uncomfortable for us or that doesn't sit quite well with us. We should ask ourselves, what if what happened to me with this person was there to send me a gift to experience something positive? If so, what would that positive thing be? It may be necessary to see things from our hearts, rather than with our heads.

Most importantly, be sure not to overlook those instances where we are at the center of causing the pain and grief inside us. We are often so quick to blame others when it may be that we are the ones who created the issue in the first place. Whether it's some incident caused by someone else or by us, the goal is to use the power of Love to heal any wounds we may have developed as children, as teens, or even as adults. By doing so, we shift into recognizing that everything that occurred in our life is something to be grateful for, rather than from a place of blame and forgiveness. While there is some benefit from experiencing the state of forgiveness initially, it is not where we always want to end up being.

> *"Heal not from the standpoint of forgiveness, but from gratitude."*

I think this point can't be overly stressed in understanding the significance of choosing to see things either from the standpoint of forgiveness or gratitude. It is extremely helpful to do so when working to heal ourselves or in realizing how others deal with their past traumas. For us to consider forgiving someone or ourselves, it is usually preceded by the feeling we've been wronged in some manner. That could only happen if we see the violation as an external attack on us, as the ego normally does. Everything from that point of view is seen as to what the other person or persons did, or what they haven't done for me.

Many self-help books explain that forgiveness is not about forgiving the person or persons that did the actual wrongdoing, but rather about helping ourselves to move forward and move on with our lives. That certainly is helpful, but it's often very hard to separate and distance ourselves from the incident itself. For some, it might take a long time to even get halfway.

Shifting into a space where authenticity and purpose reign supreme, we come to an entirely different way of seeing our "illusionary" past, transcending the concept of good and bad. Experiences of being hurt by others or ourselves are now seen in an entirely different way - as gifts to be grateful for.

At this stage, forgiveness no longer becomes the issue as it's associated with being hurt in some way. Living in pure gratitude shifts our emotional vibration to a much higher positive level of Love. A level to which we all aspire that brings reciprocal positive energy to the things we want for ourselves. I will explain later how gratitude moves us to a sort of accelerated manifestation because it helps to heal our past wounds and at the same time, brings us to a higher vibration to attract what we want for ourselves.

Some people may vehemently disagree, asking how it is possible to excuse a rapist, killer, or habitual tormentor? This seems quite reasonable and understandable living in this world of separation. Love is seen as something external to us in an ego-driven world where we choose sides. Good vs. evil, love vs. fear, us against them, you against me. In another chapter, I shall tell you a story that convinced me there is no evil in the world, only what we make it out to be.

Making the shift to recognizing our connection to the God Source, Love is internal and within each one of us, already "built-in." All experiences have the sole purpose of reminding us we live in Love. It is the reason we are here, to experience Love fully in all its various dimensions so that we can eventually share and express that Love with others. The process of using self-love on our past wounds may take a while in the healing process as we transition from ego to authenticity. This is all dependent on how much power and significance we give to our past events as a basis for defining our identity. So, take your time, love each personal experience and also those that were carried down from our parents and grandparents. This connection is often overlooked, but ancestral identity and the wounds we may silently carry forth from generation to generation is an important influential factor to consider. Wherever and however they originated, understand the purpose of this contrast; seeing it happen in our lives helps to bring enlightenment to us if we allow it to be so. Unfortunately, some of us may choose to live in this place of feeling wronged for an entire lifetime, which of course, is our choice.

A highly beneficial element in all of this is to find and join a loving and supportive group of like-minded individuals who celebrate our successes rather than tear them down. One where positive support and encouragement are normal and where everyone focuses on helping each other. A place where they "speak the same language" as in the case of author Ken Honda's Arigato Living Community, where it's centered around Ken's Happy Money philosophy.

It's not my intention to give the impression that healing our wounds and coming to a place of self-love is that simple. Some will find it easy, but for many of us, it may take a long time. It's a matter of how introspective we are in our ability to remember those challenging times and to detach ourselves from any lingering anger, hate, or bad feelings. When it's possible to make that transformation, we open ourselves to move from seeing the past as not something to forgive someone for, but to one of living in love, gratitude, and boundless possibilities. And yet, change could happen instantaneously by stepping into Who We Are and BE LOVE.

Every moment of the day, we are expressing either positive or negative energy and putting it out into the world. Regardless of which it is, the law of manifestation will bring it about. So always choose love over fear. Happiness over melancholy. And especially for those two energies, bringing them into our lives is a choice, not a given.

This is important. Loving ourselves and our past - before moving to the next step of visualizing our future, allows us to see the truth in our relationship with ourselves. By ignoring that, we spend time sabotaging our success in the process of healing. To love ourselves is to be good to ourselves. If not, we risk being fooled into believing what was coming from a place of love, actually was false and a lie. This means we take one step forward and two backward. Notice that this is not about seeing the truth about our relationship with others because that reasoning always seeks answers outside of us and perpetuates the idea that someone else is the enemy and is out of our control. So, no matter how much we try to resolve things, unless we're at peace with ourselves, there'll still be a battle raging with someone else that we feel is beyond our control to change and make better.

An example of this could be one where a person blamed their mother for not loving them as a child, as being the reason that they are now not able to have a loving relationship with someone. Seeing this from the perspective of being wronged and injured by our mother, only leaves us with lingering negative feelings where forgiveness may be the only answer to releasing the animosity held, if at all. Once we believe it is this other person who is responsible for the hurt we feel, releasing that is a challenge coming from the perspective of the ego. However, when we shift ourselves and we come from a place of seeing everything as an act born out of Love, our choice can only be one of gratitude and total release rather than practicing forgiveness.

The goal is to understand that God is Who We Are since we are part of everything. And by that extension, we are also Love. And to purposely and overtly express and experience the Love within ourselves FOR ourselves. The light we shine enlightens others and dispels their fears because once we act from the place of Love, it's meant to inspire others to be great. Discovering what true Love looks like and feels like is the first step, as we've forgotten what it was like coming from the Source. At some point, the amount of love energy will grow big enough to provide the impetus for us to start down the road to our own hero's journey.

The journey is one of self-reflection and moving into living an authentic life. Being honest with ourselves and honest with our feelings about what kind of person we want to be in this world. It's a life of feeling settled in ourselves because we now know what we want in life, and it doesn't matter what others think of us. We come to realize we're here not to convince everyone to believe in our vision, only those who choose to benefit from it.

Moving past an ego-driven life of trying to impress others, it's all about expressing the true gifts that we wish to offer. It's where the Love inside is so big that it bursts open, compelling us to share ourselves with the world. I call this "Love expressed." Others call it living their passion. Whichever it is, we experience the bliss of living this way of life filled with wanting to share our Love with what we do for others. The result is an overwhelming response of abundance to our outpouring of positive energy into the world.

Perhaps one of the most important takeaways from all of this is, have you asked yourself the question, "Do I love myself?" In an informal poll I took using a small sample of people, no one had ever asked themselves that question, but they all knew the importance of self-love. I think the better question to ask is, "Why didn't I love myself enough to ask that question before?" The answer, I believe, is that because we're so used to living in ego, we've come to believe that Love originates outside of us and we have no control over finding it. Truth of the matter is, Love has been inside us all along. All that is required of us is to look within and step into it. Without taking that action, Love will not manifest.

It's important we know what our inner dialog about Love is. What does true Love look and feel like for you? Is it telling you things to keep you from getting hurt because of what others might think? If so, that is the ego talking. True love is urging us to take the challenging road our heart has already chosen. It is the one that helps us Love ourselves and involves a commitment to the same.

> *"Fear not the road less travelled that scares you, especially when your heart has already started down that path."*

You will discover later in Chapter 7 on The Power of Gratitude and Worthiness that Love helps to accelerate the creation process once you're able to clear away all your past wounds. Again, because how we internally feel about ourselves directly connects with our self-worth and how open we are to receiving more.

Ultimately, what we strive for is to be able to say to ourselves, "I AM Love." It is quite different than us claiming that we love ourselves. To become that which we desire is to assume that identity. There is nothing else when we're finally able to fully embrace this. I am not sure if I've made this a permanent place in my life as yet, but it's what guides me each day and moment of my life.

CHAPTER THREE QUESTIONS

Take a few minutes to consider each question before answering in your journal. Write as much as you're inspired to. Review later after reading the entire book to see if your answers have changed in any significant way:

- Do you love yourself? We all know we should love ourselves, but have you ever asked yourself this question? If your answer is no, why not? If yes, explain the importance of coming to that realization.
- What are some things you have blamed others for that occurred in your past that you still hold onto? Why?
- How does it serve you to cling to blaming others from the past?
- Recall an unpleasant event you experienced in the past. Reframe it as benefiting you instead. Make a list of what those gifts would be. If you find this useful, do the same with other uncomfortable memories.

CHAPTER FOUR

FOLLOWING YOUR PASSION

The desire to move from an ego, often fear-driven life to one of authenticity, passion, and meaning, steered by Love, is essentially when the human soul begins their own hero's journey or vision quest. It's not something we need to be convinced of, but rather like a "future pull" as Dr. Wayne Dyer would describe it. It starts as a faint voice beckoning us to open ourselves up fully, to discover who we are, and what would make us happy to share with others during this lifetime. So, it's important to be alert to that faint voice of excitement.

Having newly arrived from Source when we're born, it may take us a while to get to the place where we even begin our hero's journey, if at all. It's important to remember that the ego and experiencing the illusion of separation, is necessary for us to see the contrast we're faced with, so it's never something to view negatively. Although fear plays a big part in living like this, it helps us when we realize it allows us to open ourselves up to Love. Like everything, the ego is doing its part in bringing this rich experience to us.

As the ego starts to develop, many of us will still feel a sense of connection from whence we came by just wanting to "fit in" with our peers as our identity develops. Growing up, many find the need to fit in among their friends as they begin creating these social relationships with friends and siblings. This is the process of deciding how we fit into everything around us. Depending on the influences of these early connections, some come to understand this at an early stage. But for many others, including myself, was to fit in during a period when my self-worth was beginning to develop. Looking back, all I recall was that it was painful. But I realize now that everything started with me on how I saw myself, exacerbated by fear, which is a big part of the ego.

What started with my misinterpretation of my dad's modesty about success and money as something to be ashamed of, I lived a life growing up of wanting to just blend in and "be one of the guys," playing down the benefits of my parent's hard work. Here I was trying to be like everyone else in public school, yet I had my car to drive to school at age 15 when most of my friends took the bus. How messed up was that? Should I have said no to my parents and told them I'd rather take the bus to school like all the other kids? Not on your life! To the testament of my friends though, they accepted me without question (thank you guys.) That's not to say there weren't a handful who made it a point to hurt me (thank you too, guys) but all of those episodes allowed me to come to realize we were all on a voyage of discovery, as we will be until we make our transition back to Source.

My intense desire to not be noticed and be like everyone else contrasted with my growing ego of wanting to be my own person. I tried not to bring attention to myself but often found I created situations where I did things that made me stand out from the crowd, probably intentionally. On one particular occasion, trying so hard to not call attention to myself, I signed up to skydive on one weekend with a school friend of mine. Yes, jumping out of a perfectly good airplane for the "fun" of it.

Something that my parents weren't too happy to discover afterward, because, in those days, parental consent wasn't required for a 15-year-old. Because I sort of panicked and landed wrong, I "walked" into the house with a cast on my foot, wondering how I would explain this to my mom. Since I was forced to wear a cast for weeks, the news had already spread throughout the school before I even returned; my friend who accompanied me thought it was pretty funny and told everyone. While it did offer me some notoriety in a good way, unfortunately, it didn't get me any dates, if anyone is wondering.

I guess in looking back, being the youngest of four brothers, I could find plenty of reasons for wanting to stand out. I saw it though as a maturing of the ego and at some point, the ego asserting to control my entire life. It has us believe we alone are responsible for the entire manifesting process. Using people and events outside of us to clue us into how well we're doing, how much we're progressing, and how successful we've become in comparison to others. Think about it. The whole system of grades, GPA, and winners and losers in playing sports is all about competition and comparing ourselves to others. It helps perpetuate the ego which is beneficial to our learning about life.

The problem with that is we each have unique talents and qualities and the world at that age doesn't reward uniqueness until much later in life. Being the winner is the major focus and is seen as the best measure of our competency for most of our lives, or all of our lives, unfortunately for some. In certain cases, well-meaning administrators award medals to kids coming in 5th place as a way of boosting their self-esteem. It's not until we're able to see ourselves as wonderfully unique and refuse to be measured in such a disproportionate way, do we have the courage to step into being who we are. That gives us the ability to be a happy human being full of abundance. Here again however, is another example of the duality that exists in this physical realm for our benefit. How we choose to grow through the experience is up to us.

Putting aside the type of fear we experience when in danger (which is helpful), the more insidious type is the one that often pops up when living in the ego. This type plays on our insecurities living the illusion of being separated from the God Source. We feel that we are not enough, especially when we compare ourselves to our friends or siblings, and much later in life with our co-workers. For the most part, fear is useful to help us gain perspective on the matter. While I'm not saying that we should eliminate this emotion from our lives, fear appears because we don't have enough Love inside ourselves. The whole purpose of this illusionary world is to offer contrast to us in countless rankings and contests we are exposed to and the fear that ensues. But like everything, fear helps us when we're able to choose to use the contrast for our benefit. We do that by refusing to hide behind the mask of the ego that is supposedly there to protect us and choosing instead a life of purpose, authenticity, and courageousness through vulnerability.

By following the ego where we seek outside stimuli, we're distracted from discovering true meaning. Yet it is through this process that we can become disenchanted with the status quo and seek further external rewards. Instead, it is our move inward which is how many of us start our journey. This journey may take us to far-off lands to "discover" ourselves but remember that travel and location is not a requirement. What's important is for us to open our heart to allow change. In the end, it is a change to our internal identity that's important. Having tasted this fruit of passion, we venture out for more happiness and internal contentment.

What then, is our next step? It is to commit to doing some sort of vision quest or the hero's journey I described earlier, not necessarily a formal program, but where we can release our soul to see beyond ourselves to a much greater purpose. Here is where we dig deeply into healing our wounds of the past and step away from hiding behind the mask of the insecurities of our ego. It is the ego that sets us on a path of discovery of untruths because the answers don't lie outside of us, but rather inside.

As I mentioned earlier, for some the journey could be quick, but for many of us, it will take a while. Realizing that "the journey is the reward," we can see it either as something difficult to accomplish or as an incredible adventure. If we choose to do so, and I want to remind everyone that we DO have the choice, I guarantee it will be worthwhile. Coming all this way and not being able to experience deep Love, and not sharing that with others would be an awful tragedy. Every single tear you cry today becomes another joy and happy memory in the end if you're willing to understand the purpose of this path to discovery we're all on.

I went on an actual vision quest in Death Valley, California a while back. Many things came to the surface as a result of that trek, but the most important was a deep gratitude for having this opportunity to live out this earthly experience. We join this grand "stage play" that we're all a part of in the process of expanding the universe. The experience certainly offered me a clear vision of why I was here.

During the nine days I spent in the desert with seven other people, four days and nights were alone with just a tarp over my head to protect me from the daytime sun, my sleeping bag, my journal, a pen, and enough water. Living in cities all my life, it was amazing to witness that first night alone as this fresh cool breeze passed over my face, alerting me to the impending change as the sky moved from dusk to darkness. And then in the blink of an eye, millions upon millions of stars burst onto the scene all around me leaving me in complete awe. This feeling of being insignificantly small, and yet offering me a tiny glimpse of where we all came from and the miracle which we call "creation."

When it was all over, we broke camp to resettle at a campground next to a small motel in the town of Stovepipe Wells. After paying a couple of dollars to use the shower facilities next to the pool, our small group adjourned to the restaurant for our first meal since the four-day fast. As I sat there with everyone talking and laughing, I was overcome with a deep sense of gratitude for being in the presence of this group of friends, who were mere strangers just several days earlier. I teared up, unable to answer a fellow quester asking me if everything was alright. It wasn't. Something inside of me changed that day, thinking if I died tomorrow, I'd be okay because I had come not only to be touched by Love but worthy of Love. Love for myself and the universe around me. In looking back, I see now how the overwhelming feelings of gratitude during this experience enhanced my life. It gave me purpose. It gave me Love and it gave me a greater sense of worth. Enough to share it with you all reading this book. Whatever the source of that gratitude, the result is the same. It gives us a sense of a feeling worthy of being loved and in turn, expands what we believe we deserve to receive in this world. The key to healing our abundance.

*"The greater the feeling of gratitude,
the more profound healing we experience."*

Episodes like these move us to discover more about what our reason is for being here. No, it's not to be born, then having parents, siblings, friends, and enemies making our life a hell. Perhaps never forgiving them for what they did to us and then struggling at making a living and then dying. Or the idea to work our asses off trying to pay for that brand-new car we bought three months ago, that we thought would bring us everlasting joy.

Ultimately, it's this movement away from living an ego-driven life of fear, long-held attachments to wounds of the past, and struggle, to one that opens the door to authentic purpose through remembering our connection to Source and Love. Many situations encourage or push us to begin our trek, but it usually begins with an uneasy feeling to experience more. When interviewing people about this, most will say, "I don't know, I just felt like there was something more to life than what I was doing," or they'd ask, "Is this all there is?"

All along, I've pointed out the importance of moving from an ego-driven life to one of purpose through the process of self-love. While moving from ego to purpose is purely optional and some may choose not to undertake it during this lifetime, chances are you are searching for answers or have already departed on your journey or quest. Remember that healing our wounds and traumas from the past will take time, but our willingness to take the necessary steps is a sure sign we've started on this transformational trip.

There is no preparation for it, all that is required is the desire to make the shift of wanting more meaning in our lives and honesty about Who We Are. Begin by asking ourselves what brings us joy and satisfaction when we're able to do it. What is something that if someone asked you about you could end up talking to them for hours and hours and not notice the time? What brings you a satisfying feeling when you share it with someone else? It's important to look inward for the rewards rather than externally. This is the key to a purpose-driven life when purpose becomes our prime motivator.

*"The human journey of the soul's desire for fulfillment
begins when we discover what we love to do in life
and feel that profound desire
to share that deep love with others."*

Does this mean we will never encounter fear anymore? No, of course not. But we now understand the purpose of fear as a way of discovering the answer to help us on our journey. When fear, anger, anxiety, and sadness appear, understand them for what they represent, and allow yourself to transcend the hurt to emerge onto the other side. It is useful to provide breakthroughs. There is so much truth in the quote, "Feel the fear and do it anyway." Just remember that everything is a choice, not a consequence. Visit the place where we become empowered by seeing things from the perspective of Love; it opens up new pathways to understanding what's holding us back. This is why when we work through our past wounds, from wherever they originated, clarity envelops us and our heart opens up.

Understanding the why of something, while offering insight, is less important than what and how. What can I do to change this and help me move forward? How can I make this happen? Release all expectations.

"Design your dream, then let go and let God."

The root of passion is found by developing a true Love for what we wish to express here in this dimension. It's that simple, but not without effort. Probably the biggest effort is the movement from ego to an authentic purpose-driven life. The quicker you do, the easier it becomes, because we move from external cues to internal ones. First, fall in love with what you wish to express by falling in love with yourself. We do this by discovering what Love feels and looks like and we accept it into ourselves to help us work out our past wounds. With this comes the clarity of what will truly bring us joy. Have a clear picture of what it will look like and most importantly, what it will feel like in great detail, then live it now. Talk and act as though it happened. If our mind has already experienced it, any possible fear attached to it disappears, because we believe it's already happened in our physical world. Because there is so much fear associated with an illusionary future, that it often feels safer to stay where we are, even if it's a more painful place to be. This often manifests as procrastination or self-sabotage which we will devote a separate chapter to.

Remember that life is like a balancing act, between making things happen by way of our physical efforts and the power of spiritual manifestation. We shall also cover this topic in a later chapter. Suffice to say though, we are so entrenched with the illusion of ego and separateness and that breeds fear and scarcity. While it may sound silly to say this, as spiritual beings, it's important to always remember to do our part in this dance of creation we have with God.

Physical action is part of the process of bring about what we want and desire. Therefore, all the magic we are expecting to take place has to have a corresponding physical energy to be expended. First to act, feel, and BE in this future self of ours; then to detach from the outcome and just trust, and finally to take the physical action when the opportunity presents itself.

So, how do we identify with who we are? This is the nature of the quest and journey we've decided to embark on. A true identification comes from being in this place of purpose because the meaning of Who We Are arises from a place deep within our heart out of Love. It is not associated with the route of the ego that some of us choose to stay on. That road is driven by what we believe others want for us or what we think is the "common sense" thing to do. Frankly, with all of our gifts and talents, it's unlikely any of us came here to be common.

Many of us choose jobs and careers because they'll bring us a lot of money, thinking that's the answer to complete happiness. Others do it out of a sense of obligation because it was something associated with past generations. External pressures of obligation or our need to appear successful in the eyes of others, all arise in the world of the ego. The future pull to express Who We Are does not apply in that world. However, working from obligation could certainly be one that eventually becomes one of purpose.

The ego may fight tooth and nail to keep us in this externally competitive world. This is part of the hero's journey, where we encounter the metaphorical dragon of doubt and fear. Detoxifying, the walking away from the lingering effects of the illusionary world, requires more self-love and feelings of worthiness. That is, to purposely and fully express and experience the Love within ourselves and for ourselves, knowing we deserve all that we are creating. That we're worthy of Love and worthy of all that we desire. This helps us to then begin establishing new associations for ourselves, both from the standpoint of what we should be doing as well as what we shouldn't be doing. Ultimately, the measure is how deeply this passion that we want to express to the world resonates in our hearts – helping to heal ourselves and heal others that we touch.

When we reach the point in our journey that we've slayed our dragon and are confident as to what we want to share with others, we step forward into the place of BEING. By this point, there's a certain confidence and anticipation that becomes apparent. It's important to remember that we possessed everything when we arrived here from Source for what we've chosen to do. All the courage, all the talent, whatever it might be, we possess, coming into this life to step into what brings us the most joy. While the concept of BEING may be a bit difficult for many of us to practice, it's important to remember that this is a natural state for us living in Source. We are experiencing the greatest expression of ourselves as a part of God, but somehow, we've forgotten that. Nevertheless, stepping into Who You Are could be another journey in itself.

Formal education or skills training is part of preparing us for this point if we wish to be a doctor or craftsperson, but I'm not speaking of that. Rather, it's about reaching a point where Love becomes everything that we are to express and share with the world. It's the moment we recognize it's time. The time to express ourselves to the world so others can benefit from our Love of what we're doing, again, this thing I call, "Love expressed."

Having moved out of living through our ego and now purpose-driven, we must realize there is no place to get to because there is no place to go. Understand everything that we fear has already been experienced and expressed already by us. There's nothing to learn. Move forward knowing that you already have been living this dream of yours and all the answers are inside of you already. This is "expectation with confidence." Fear of expression and rejection is replaced by the passion of your soul. There is nothing more important.

Your journey is for others and the benefit of God to continually experience and express that which we are and for the benefit of expanding the universe. Speak your truth to the people who wish to hear it. Their journey might be quite different, and no one knows what path that person is on, even the person themselves. Be there to remind them of the significance of making it this far and send them off with Love.

CHAPTER FOUR QUESTIONS

Take a few minutes to consider each question before answering in your journal. Write as much as you're inspired to. Review later after reading the entire book to see if your answers have changed in any significant way.

- Do you remember a time in your childhood when you just wanted to fit in and be accepted? Explain that time of your life. Did you speak and act in a manner that just wasn't who you were?
- Would you say you prefer to be like everyone else and not stand out in the crowd or be unique? Why do you think you're that way?
- Have you gone on your own quest for vision? If so, what did you learn from it? If not, what answers would you be seeking if you did?
- How important do you think it is to follow what your inner self is telling you to do?

CHAPTER FIVE
LOSS, DEATH AND SEPARATION

In the previous chapters, we have reviewed our journey from Source, the place of complete Unconditional Love. We are then born into this illusionary plane of existence where we experience separation and contrast. In this way, we decide how we want our lives to play out, all for the benefit of expanding the Universe. We can use our ego to guide us in how we live or choose a path where we are driven by purpose and authenticity. Living via your ego will always be a more challenging endeavor because, in that state, we constantly depend on things external to ourselves for solutions, answers, and our self-worth. So, when it comes to issues relating to loss, answers are more difficult to come by and harder to make sense of.

The ultimate experience of separation is loss and death. We must remember loss and death in this world are only illusions, but understandably, extremely painful when faced with it, not knowing its true purpose. It could be something as devastating as a series of deaths, perhaps of our grandmother, father, sister, or best friend, all within a couple of years. Or it could be having to euthanize our beloved pet that has given us so much unconditional love for so many years. Both are painful events, to say the least.

I do not trivialize these experiences nor the grief they bring, as I lost both my parents and a brother. These personal experiences were all too real and painful when they occurred. However, we must understand that all of our negative emotions allow us to experience a contrasting emotional vibration. It is through that experience that we can move into becoming stronger, and more courageous, having more gratitude for other people, and a host of other empowering things. Certain deeper levels of gratitude connect us with our ultimate goal as it relates to Love and Abundance. Or we can choose to live with extreme sadness, despair, anger, and other negative emotional vibrations. Both are useful for us to experience in this big stage play we are a part of called life.

Keep in mind that some souls will come here specifically to experience these negative feelings and vibrations of loss to understand and know their corresponding positive vibrations of Love. This is accomplished with the help of other incarnates through the process of loss and death, either as an infant or child death. As hard as it may be to read this, it brings purpose to their brief time on this illusionary stage. And because everything in this universe is an energy vibration, nothing can or will die. It just changes in its vibrational form. All the religious texts speak of the soul going on and never dying, yet at this stage, our time is brief, so it's important to make the best of it.

Understandably, all loss, however minor, helps us to understand and decide how we wish to act and appear to others. Losing our keys and wallet with all our credit cards could evoke anger at oneself for being so careless, frustration knowing our life is interrupted by our negligence, or even fear that someone who finds them might create criminal acts with our information.

Choosing to not live by way of our ego recognizes that everything has a purpose and that death, and other such loss, is but an illusion. It requires us to choose whether to change or live with it, for however long we choose to do so. Since we live in this paradoxical world of contrast, what the experience with death and loss can help us remember is "Love." Strive to embrace the side of Love in understanding this experience of loss and your life will be profoundly changed through this knowledge.

Years ago, I had a lot of questions about death and dying, as my parents were in their mid-eighties. Although my mother transitioned at age 95 and my father two months short of 101 years old, I felt compelled to read and study as much material on the subject of death and dying, as I could find. I was hesitant at first, but something told me this was something that could help me to ultimately ease the pain I would surely face. Most significant was Elisabeth Kübler-Ross's classic, *On Death and Dying*, and her autobiography, *The Wheel of Life,* plus *The Tibetan Book of the Dead*. All of this started me down the path to the enlightenment of what many of us are too afraid to speak about or contemplate. I recall reading one such book that I can't remember the title or author, but it essentially saw the death experience as a way for us to gain perspective on living a very purposeful and happy life. I wondered how this was possible when faced with such permanence at a devastating time in our lives. Yet what these books and those that followed instilled in me, was that when we come to embrace loss, the opposite happens. We discover the only thing important in all of this, and that is to experience and express Love. That's it.

Another thing that was both a help and an honor, was when I decided to become a hospice volunteer to provide respite to families for their dying loved ones. It was a way of preparing for my parents' eventual passing. While there was much ambivalence and fear of doing so in the beginning, it freed me from past indoctrinations of religious teachings. In addition, it offered me new insights as to our purpose in being here. There is a beauty in caring for the dying that remarkably has brought so much joy and appreciation into my life. It's hard to describe, but it helped me to appreciate my life, myself, and everyone around me that I knew – and didn't know.

There was one patient I sat with every Saturday for 13 months before he made his transition, which changed my perception quite a bit. During my time with him, he taught me so much about his journey as he edged closer to death. At times, he would have brief moments of being connected to Source when at age 96, he saw his two deceased brothers who died when they were 27 and 35 smiling down at him waiting patiently. Whether they were hallucinations or his reality, really didn't matter because it brought comfort and happiness to him in the months before his passing over.

Some people think it admirable for me to have the courage to sit with the dying, but really, I see now that the experience turned out to be a profound blessing that changed me forever. I can see why some would think that, but admiration was not what I was seeking – rather answers. I found a profound, spiritual gratitude. I look back now and wonder whether that was similar to my vision quest experience that I spoke about earlier.

Hospice taught me that the fear I had about death and dying was unfounded. Rather, I came to realize how important this transitional period is that all of us will go through at some point in our lives. For some, it could be extremely quick, while for others like my patient, a much longer process. I've come to believe that if we can strive to live an authentic life, then we can certainly also die authentically. It's a time when most people no longer have any reason to live behind the masks of their egos and can express themselves as the joyous, authentic souls they were meant to be.

This was also the time when I had a lot of questions that very few could answer to my satisfaction. So, I started a non-grief death and dying discussion group called, "Pauhana." In Hawaii, we colloquially use that term to mean the end of a workday or workweek and to relax, now that the week is over. There are a lot of other wonderful grief-based support groups, but nothing focused on a straightforward non-grief discussion about death and dying. In its few years of existence, it attracted a lot of amazing people with very interesting and helpful insights that enlightened and comforted all who attended. We covered topics such as the greatest fears people worry about in the dying process, home funerals, near-death experiences, and everything in between. As an idea of how we viewed dying, one of our group members who most people would characterize as having a slightly morbid sense of humor remarked,

"You know death is so fashionable! Everybody's doing it!"

From these experiences, certain truths opened up for me. On one such meeting of Pauhana, I secured a video of author Dr. Jean Houston, and played it for the group to discuss. In it, she was recalling her time with her Italian grandmother who was in a coma, when suddenly, she awoke from her deep state of unconsciousness and began speaking Italian to her late husband. This was her native tongue, so it was nothing unusual, except for the fact that she believed her husband was in the room with her in spirit and began to have a conversation with him. What was interesting though was during the video, Jean noticed the grandmother was particularly happy and asked her why. Her grandmother went on to tell her she was comforted by what was to come, in "crossing over." When Jean asked her to describe what she saw, her grandmother told her with a smile that it looked like, "a party was going on over there."

That weekend, I visited my hospice patient, who I had gotten pretty close to by this time, enough for me to ask him if he too could see over to the other side and if so, what it looked like. Without hesitation, he replied, "Yes," and then paused for a few moments to try to describe it, and said, "Well, it kind of looks like there's a party going on over there!" Chills went through my body hearing him use the same words that Houston's grandmother had said to her. Something good was happening over there that we were unaware was occurring.

After that incident and in discussing this matter with others, I have come to the belief that people nearing their transition are very close to a sheer veil of vibration between them and the Source. They can see over there and instinctively know when they move through the veil, they will no longer live in this illusionary world of separation. We of the "living," being so far away from the veil, can only see the opaqueness of the separation because we are vibrating at a different level. Whether this is true or not, I don't know, but the whole experience provided another piece of the puzzle in my understanding of life and death. Perhaps the one thing we might be afraid of in all of this is what our answers will be when we return to Source and we are asked, "Did you experience and express Love fully while you were there, and did you have fun?" If your answer would be no to either question, then what are you waiting for?

My search for knowledge also led me to attend a convention of IANDS, the International Association of Near-Death Studies, that "just happened" to be holding their convention in my hometown that year. This wonderful organization helped me expand my understanding of our existence here. I informally interviewed about 30 people who had actual near-death experiences, which later helped me with my hospice work. Most importantly, it helped me lose my fear of death. I chatted with one gentleman who explained to me that he no longer feared dying and when I asked him why, he told me that he saw life as an unbroken, continuous circle of birth and death, birth and death.

From that point on, it all made sense to me, especially when all of the other puzzle pieces fell into place. All along though, I wondered about the true reason we are all here and why we live in a world of such conflict and disagreement. The answer, of course, was to help us decide how we want to live based on these contrasting experiences.

In all of that, I think the one true gift we can give our parents or those making the transition is our full loving presence during their dying process, no matter how difficult it may seem. We all will eventually experience the movement from form to formless. If there is such a thing as "living authentically", then why can we not "die authentically" as well? We give honor to those making this final journey back to spirit by trying to set aside our grief if only temporarily. Death is such a difficult issue to deal with I know. However, when we're able to see death as not an end but as a continuation, there might be hope for us. It helps us emerge from the so-called darkness of sorrow and onto the other side of reasoning, so we can open ourselves up to a profound change. We discover the true meaning of Love and life and what our deepest passions are that we came here to do. In other words, tragedy often creates the space for us to discover who we truly are meant to be.

Most people working in hospice know that when people take their last breath of life, a high percentage will choose to die when no one is in the room - meaning they choose to die when the person sitting with them leaves the room for a few moments. So, it's a privilege to be able to be present when a person transitions over. I'm led to believe that the dying do know if the person(s) they're leaving behind, can emotionally handle that passage. There are many accounts of a loved one passing just minutes after they've been told by their adult children, that it's okay for them to move on and that they will be okay with them leaving. There are so many stories of this type, that it seems unbelievable.

Knowing this, I was so fortunate to be there for both my parents' transitions with a presence of unconditional Love. For them, this is what I described earlier as the process of "dying authentically." It is having the presence of mind to help them make their exit with ease while other friends and family members are trying to cope with the situation. This is an important moment we will all experience at some point. For some, this process of dying could take quite a while – for others it occurs quickly. Here is where we slowly lose all sense of space and time and as we transition over, the role of the ego or the importance of the "I and Other" disappear, as we move back into Source and the All There Is. It is simply the completion of the soul's temporary journey here from birth to death and every delicious moment in between if we so choose to embrace it.

I still miss my parents and brother dearly when I'm feeling detached from Spirit. But I am reminded of what I experienced and my time with them here, what they helped me realize, and the Love they shared with me. I also believe they are always with me and around me, just in a different vibrational form.

Loss is fundamental to our physical human development in that sometimes we must lose something, or rid ourselves of it, to make space for something brand new to come into our lives. This is why for many of us, a new job may be offered, or money that was nowhere to be found suddenly appears. This act of surrendering is important because as individuals, we have the belief that we control everything with our own doing, which is not true. It also can be a signal that we're ready to move to the next step - the one that we're unsure of making but afraid to move into.

"Surrendering allows us to move on and move up."

Surrendering is also a key component of manifestation, as we will discuss later. Surrendering to a situation is such an important concept to remember and utilize, whenever we face something where we find ourselves stuck and lost, no matter how many things we've tried to do to change it. There is a lot of wisdom in the recovery movement's mantra, "Let go and let God," especially when faced with some type of loss, making us feel incapacitated. But if we're not prepared to be open to change and use an alternative path, the opportunity for discovery of a possible new path will not be within our reach.

One night during my vision quest in Death Valley, I dreamt I was trying to get beyond a wall but was unable to. My face was pushed up against the barrier and no matter how hard I tried, I couldn't even budge it. In the dream, I heard the words, "relax and surrender," so I stopped pushing. As I did and backed off from the obstruction that I was continuously frustrated with, I realized the wall was only three feet/one-meter wide, which allowed me to easily walk around it. Had I not surrendered to the notion of getting through the barrier in what my ego told me was the "logical" way, I wouldn't have discovered to listen to my intuition and just walk around it. We often believe there is only one way to get through something because it's more expedient, but it often fails us as we discover this alternate route. What may have been seen as taking a detour, or the longer path, was the quicker way. If you are like me, constantly reading and studying different methods of resolving a problem, yet unable to find the solution, then relax. The answer will come to you, telling us it's time to "move on and move up." There is nothing else to do and nothing else to learn but to BE.

Let me make it clear that this is not the same as "giving up," as "surrendering" is often a prelude to major changes happening for us. So, we use this feeling to our advantage as a way of reminding ourselves that negative events are always something to bless, not reject. The more we dwell on the rejection, the more we bring all the negative unwanted vibrations that we associate with that notion.

I am reminded of a story a friend once told me of a woman he counseled. He was a hospice grief counselor where this woman's husband had transitioned over a year ago. One day, she announced to my friend that she would no longer be attending grief sessions because she was ready to move on. While delighted, he asked her what had happened to cause this change. She went on to tell him that she had a dream of her husband coming to her, sitting next to her bedside, and telling her to stop the grieving and to move on. He then gave her a beautiful unique-looking pendant as a gift. The next morning while having breakfast in the kitchen before going to work, her grandson ran in and excitedly said, "Grandma,

Grandma...I saw Grandpa last night!" To which the woman asked the grandson to tell her what he saw. The boy said he saw his grandfather sitting at her bedside talking to her but then was told, "Go back to bed!" by the elder man, and he promptly did. The story was hard to believe but she took it at face value.

Later at work that day, a co-worker told the woman she wanted to give her a little gift, something that she saw in the store that she thought she'd like. It turned out to be the same pendant that her husband had gifted to her in her dream the night before. Naturally, she took this to be an important message not to ignore – that it was time to surrender and stop grieving. It became clear to her that her late husband may not be there in physical form anymore, but that he indeed was still around her. Surrender allowed her to move on with her life, which is what all of those who leave before us want us to do. The meaning behind "move on and move up" is telling us to "move up" emotionally with positive thoughts. It is not about no longer loving that person and/or feeling guilty.

Death and loss are–but a myth in this illusionary world of ours, where we have to navigate and find meaning, if we are willing to seek it. It is all about the discovery of the magnificent story we write for ourselves on a moment-to-moment basis. It is by our choices and through overcoming perceived adversity from the concepts of death, dying, separation, and loss, that is the true reward.

CHAPTER FIVE QUESTIONS

Take a few minutes to consider each question before answering in your journal. Write as much as you're inspired to. Review later after reading the entire book to see if your answers have changed in any significant way.

- Write a short paragraph of what you learned from losing some highly valued object or thing like a job. Loss and separation always lead us to just the opposite by opening doors we once thought were closed.
- Write about a time when you were constantly faced with an immovable barrier, only to surrender to it, which allowed you to "walk around it" instead. What did it teach you?
- Surrendering to the loss of someone you love is not about the guilt of not loving them anymore. If you hold onto that attachment, explain why. If not, what changed?
- Recall a time that someone close to you has died. This could be someone in your family,

a close friend or beloved pet. After coming through the sorrow and grief, what are some of the things that has helped you experience being a better human being today?

CHAPTER SIX
VIBRATIONAL REALITY

In case you haven't heard, it is believed that everything in the Universe is vibration. Quantum mechanics has proven that we are all connected, where separation does not exist, nor does time and space. Our senses though, tell us otherwise. The magnificent thing is we are not some random quantum soup of unrelated incidences and occurrences, but like the beautiful performance of a grand symphony masterpiece, with each of us playing our unique part with our unique type of instrument in perfect harmony. The problem is that so many of us only show up for the rehearsals and keep practicing and practicing, but not many for the actual performances, afraid to let others hear the beautiful music they can make when they are following their purpose.

Many of us still have a difficult time accepting the fact that we are all clusters of vibrating particles, all connected within this amazing universe of ours. The truth of the matter, every particle affects every other particle in varying degrees. However, all we see and believe is that we are separate human bodies interacting independently of each other. So, we make plans, ignore our inner voice, and come up with what we think will bring us satisfaction and probable happiness. We are born into this world and try to make sense of it, playing along with what most people do by going to school, getting a job, marrying, having children, retiring, and living as long as possible – until we die. The hope is that we experience some meaningful measure of joy occasionally. In reality, though, we are all vibrational and emotionally driven beings coming from the Source, but now existing in the state of a lower frequency and trying to understand it all and make it work for us.

All vibrations and emotions are energy and as physical objects, we are putting out that energy continuously in everything we do, even during our sleeping

ABUNDANT SOUL ABUNDANT LIFE

hours. Being in the physical body, we are essentially vibrating at a lower rate of energy than a thought or desire, which are less dense. Lower vibrations include things like humans and other objects that seem solid for the most part; with very high frequency things being invisible to our naked eye. All energy keeps changing its form by way of our feelings and, like our souls, it never dies. Positive and negative emotions create corresponding energy vibrations with positive feelings vibrating at a higher frequency and negative feelings at lower frequencies. In what may seem to be illusionary to define and perceive within our physical world, our feelings offer us a way to deal with the separation we all experience with each other and with things like money and abundance. It is important to recognize that money, while appearing to be seemingly real in terms of currency, is an emotional thought vibration as is everything in this Universe.

Because we live in this vibrational quantum soup, we are affected by other people's actions whether personally or from afar, and we in turn influence others in the same manner. When we put out similar frequency vibrations, our positive vibrational energy attracts all of the good things we want for ourselves, essentially things that match our frequency of emotions. These can be wonderful situations we wish to occur, people who are similar to us, and positive feelings we hope to experience. Think of it like a radio or television where we tune into specific channels that we want to watch or listen to. We are like the tuner in these devices that help bring us into the correct frequency. If we wish to bring money into our lives, our corresponding beliefs and emotional feelings about it should align and match. Therefore, if we have negative associations with wealth and money, what we think will help us, will not manifest. Consequently, it is these same negative or low energy vibrations that will bring us the things we fear if we stay in that low and more dense vibration.

Simply put, both positive and negative feelings about something, align us with-people, things, and situations, whether good or bad of similar vibrational rates of energy. This is the basis of the Law of Attraction, introduced by William Atkinson and made famous by the spiritual entity Abraham and Esther and Jerry Hicks. Or the "Law of Assumption" brought forward by Neville Goddard. He believed whatever we felt as true for ourselves, brings it into our lives. Both have their roots in quantum physics, and we shall go into this in more detail in the chapter on Manifestation.

Happiness, joy, peace, and not surprisingly, Love, all vibrate at a high rate, which is certainly understandable given our state of energy and feelings when we're experiencing these emotions. Whereas anger, guilt, sorrow, and fear bring us down to a lower frequency rate. Not surprisingly, when we're feeling sad, we describe it as "feeling down" and our physical body takes on the appearance of slumping shoulders and head lowered, but when we're happy, we stand tall and upright and feel like "jumping for joy," hands outstretched.

While it is said that the human body at rest has a particularly low vibrational state, measurements for forgiveness, as well as the act of gratitude and Love, are much higher. The actual frequency numbers are irrelevant for this discussion, except to say positive emotions help us bring forth the things we want most in our lives.

Vibrational energy is real, and I have a personal experience to share that proved it to me. This happened quite a while ago when a friend of mine asked me to join her for 'table tipping" at a friend's house. Thinking I already knew how to tip a server at a restaurant, I wasn't keen on going, as I was feeling a bit under the weather. I had developed a headache, along with upper respiratory congestion and fatigue. My friend told me that table tipping was something quite different - like a Ouija board on steroids. I was both intrigued and skeptical, and therefore made it a point of going anyway.

When we arrived, there must have been over 30 people crowded around a bunch of tables. I was invited to take a seat at one of them and we were instructed to place both of our hands flat on the table. Almost immediately, the table lifted itself onto two of its four legs and suspended itself. No one was holding it up and everyone had both hands lightly placed on top. I was amazed and dumbfounded at the same time. Then the gentleman who "hosted" the table explained we could all ask one yes or no question. If the answer was no, the table would "tap" the floor once, and if yes, then twice. As each person took their turn and asked their question, the table would 'reply" either with a light tap or two or a forceful response, to indicate a definitive answer. It was truly bizarre.

When it came to my turn, I told the host to skip me, as I wasn't feeling very well. Instead of doing so, he instructed me to put both of my hands back on the table. At that point, he asked all of the people at the table to send me healing energy through the table. As soon as he said that my hands began to become warm, lasting for about a minute. Less than 15 minutes later my headache disappeared, my nose cleared and all the congestion was gone; it was as if I wasn't sick at all. How all of the tapping, lifting, and lowering occurred with the table, I can't explain. But I do not doubt the power we all possess through those vibrations of love and caring sent to me that evening.

It's not surprising then that the practice of reiki has become so popular as a healing modality. Reiki is the Japanese practice of using the practitioner's energy to help heal their patient. Whether it is an acceptable form of treating certain problems, there is a no doubt in my mind of the power to affect others and some sort of energy is present.

The Chinese have long known the existence and practice of the energy of qi (chi) in many applications. The awareness and practice of qigong in Chinese history dates back over 4,000 years. Qigong is about movement and healing. More specifically, the movement of energy and was part of traditional Chinese medicine. Its main goal was focused on health maintenance and wellness.

However, it found it's place in the various forms of martial arts including Tai Chi.

Within the Japanese martial art form of Aikido, which translates loosely to the way to harmonize energy, it uses qi. A good friend who practices it told me a story in which he witnessed a very old grandmaster from Okinawa doing a demonstration of this unseen energy. They had two big men, each of whom was almost twice the weight of this older gentleman, run towards him. Before they could even get close, he waved his hand down to his side in a sweeping motion. The result was that the two young men fell to the side - brushing them to the side with his energy without him physically laying a hand on either of them. So, the power of our vibrational energy should not be dismissed or underestimated, as it forms the basis for spiritual manifestation.

Any person can figure out that staying in a positive frame of mind or emotional frequency will attract what we wish, but the question is how does one get that way? Especially when so many negative things are happening around us, the rent is due in a week with no way to pay it, or someone close to us has died. We shall go more into this in the chapter specifically focused on Manifestation.

Because we live under the illusion of time, acute occurrences will take a while because it's difficult to move from an extremely negative vibration to a positive one. There are obvious exceptions of course. But say one was depressed and feeling powerlessness, which are both near the bottom of our emotional frequency. It is difficult to just jump up to a positive state of joy but rather we must make intermediate steps to just get to a place of neutrality and boredom. Understand that within this physical realm, it takes time, and each time we experience the same adversity, we're able to cope with it better. In addition, when we recognize that all of our experiences are for our benefit, the transition from negative emotions to positive ones becomes a lot quicker. This discussion is meant to make you aware of the concept and reality of what we can't see. The vibrational reality of this space we occupy.

Many people have written about the multiple ways to raise our vibration. First and foremost is to spend time around a lot of other people who are joyous, happy, peaceful, and passionate about their lives. A supportive group of people will help when times are tough and keep us accountable for our progress toward our dreams. These types of people live mainly in a higher emotional and vibrational state than others. For those of us who are afraid and want to play it small, having others as models for what is possible is very important.

We've all had situations where we're influenced by our friends and cohorts, so be sure to pick good ones that help inspire you. We all have something inside of us that we want to share but have become so fearful because of our past traumas. So often, the people we think will support us like our families turn out to be our worse critics for our dreams. Choose to not let that happen and make it a point to find like-minded people.

Find people who act from their heart rather than from their ego, while we work on loving ourselves and healing our past wounds. I have mentioned previously about author Ken Honda's Arigato Living Community where I've personally found an extremely supportive group of individuals and an environment to help upgrade our thinking about creating abundance for ourselves using Ken's Happy Money principles.

This does not mean that some people may not still be acting from their ego as they discover their way. Just keep in mind, our emotional vibrations will attract the same type of people energetically, as what we're putting out. When we do encounter others incongruent to ourselves, ask whether it's because our energy is attracting that kind of unwanted vibration, or if this is a way to show us the contrast so we can be clear of our intentions to act differently.

Another way to indirectly raise our vibrations is to meditate, practice qigong or other breathing exercises, or spend time in nature. These practices will help quiet the mind and clear out the clutter when focusing on the manifestation process.

Despite what some people have us believe that we must do meditation a certain specific way, the truth is there are many, many different ways. The idea is to just start and make it a habit because meditation raises our resting vibrational level to make it easier to align with higher frequencies the more we practice it. We will talk later about the part of the mind that meditation can be very helpful in connecting with Spirit.

But for now, start meditating about 1 to 2 minutes per session so there's no pressure. By doing so, inspired thoughts will come to us easier during the day. Of course, we must pay attention because, in the beginning, those messages are faint. But the more and more we quiet our mind, the clearer and more discernible it becomes. Spirit is always answering us. We just can't hear it because we have too much chatter going on in our heads.

I first learned how to meditate by walking in the park without judgment. This means to see a tree or a sunset and suspend any thoughts about how beautiful it looked momentarily and just turn away and focus on something else. I discovered by doing this consistently, I was able to clear my mind so on days when I couldn't go out, closing my eyes would produce the same result.

Personally, I've discovered journaling has helped me shift my vibration. Obviously, it's not for everyone. However, throughout the years, the silent conversation with myself has convinced me God and my guides are always listening and trying to find ways to communicate with me. At some point, I noticed I was no longer the source of the brilliance I thought I was developing. It was, however, that my vibration had raised to a level where I could now hear the message. It's important to remember that as we go about creating, to listen to the wise voice inside ourselves. Stop trying to do the things you feel is the way it's supposed to happen. As the wise saying goes, "Let go and let God."

Finally, have as a goal to live in joy and happiness every day - which leads us to discovering our bliss. I shall discuss the topic of bliss later because it's that important in healing the abundance in our lives. Focusing on living in joy and happiness changes our vibrational state and helps us to appreciate the things we've accomplished.

CHAPTER SIX QUESTIONS

Take a few minutes to consider each question before answering in your journal. Write as much as you're inspired to. Review later after reading the entire book to see if your answers have changed in any significant way.

- Have you experienced a certain negative event repeatedly and if so, has it gotten easier over time? If so, how has that impacted your confidence with that and other challenges you face?
- Do you meditate, do breathing exercises, or spend time in nature? If not, create a new vision for yourself that includes these practices and then commit to changing.
- Be open to learning about the energy we all possess inside ourselves and our ability to heal others. Explore on the internet at least one of these mediums (qigong, reiki, tai chi, etc.) and share your experience with others.
- Keep a journal of your meditation practice noting any sensations and changes in awareness you're experiencing.

CHAPTER SEVEN
THE POWER OF GRATITUDE AND WORTHINESS

The principles of forgiveness, gratitude, and worthiness are key elements in healing our abundance. Let me say that again to reemphasize this. How much we value ourselves directly influences how much we feel we deserve. And by that extension, what manifests for us in this world. This was addressed in earlier chapters, however, we will now look at it much more in-depth, because it deserves to be fully understood.

But first, another personal experience that shaped my understanding of life, as it relates to helping us understand forgiveness and hopefully how to transcend it. When I had the opportunity to interview several people who had gone through a near-death experience (NDE) in that IANDS Conference I mentioned earlier, I met at least a half dozen people who had told me of a relatively similar encounter that I'm about to tell you. During their "out-of-body" journey, they described meeting their "spirit or soul family." These are usually about a dozen or so souls whom we energetically resonate with on a mental, physical, emotional, and spiritual level, bonded by Love. They are individual souls who agree to assist each other in whatever experience we each wish to accomplish during our lifetimes here. In one lifetime, they are maybe our parents or siblings—in other lifetimes they may serve us in the role of a perpetrator/tormentor or a sworn enemy. Or they could be a soul that agrees to spend a brief time here to allow a person to experience the grief and sorrow of their child or infant dying. While it may be difficult to accept, all of this is done out of Love as there is nothing else but Unconditional Love in Source.

While none of their stories were exactly the same, they all were told that their soul family was bonded by Love. Their willingness to play the various roles, whether good or bad, all came out of that Love. Two had witnessed a group meeting of their soul family whereby they were asking for "volunteers" to play certain roles to help this particular person having the NDE to have a certain encounter. In both cases, it was explained to them that all of the most significant people we meet here in this "illusional" stage play of ours, agreed to do so at our request. Both people I interviewed understood immediately who this person was in their lives, although everything was more or less light energy, and they couldn't see their faces. They later realized the significance of why they were shown this in that it was to help them understand the traumatic experience they had a difficult time releasing. All experiences originate from our wish to experience a certain event enriched by the contrast with at its core the expression of Love. Spirit or God Consciousness does not contain evil. Evil is a human construct brought about by illusory separation.

I relate my encounters with these people because they offered me an insight into understanding why certain things are. From this space, I was able to shift to moving out of my ego self, who would always look to others as to the reason for the bad things that happened in my life. All along, I was the one who was responsible as it was my wish before arriving here. This may not sit well with some of you reading this. I urge you to be open to this notion. The alternative could be a long fraught life with hate and unforgiveness. Not for the perpetrator but towards yourself.

My goal here is to point out how important it is for us to move from an ego-based world which lays the foundation for this separated physical realm, to one of authenticity, where we're being honest and true to ourselves through purpose. While not everyone will do so and may spend an entire lifetime living by way of their ego, that's their choice and it is the correct one for them if that is what they wish. The challenge is their constant reliance on others to form the basis for how successful they are, so the healing process from past wounds becomes much more difficult. Lingering feelings of indiscretions by people from the past could still haunt them despite how many times they say, "I love you," in the mirror to themselves.

While forgiveness certainly places high on the emotional frequency chart, I believe it could also exist in a lower, more dense vibration if we still cling to our wounds from the past. Perhaps we still cling to certain lingering resentment toward the person(s) or situations that we believed hurt us. This is especially true if these negative associations sit hidden, deep within us in our subconscious mind. Be that as it may, it could also be a positive one if we're able to transcend those hurtful wounds.

While I'm sure there are instances when some can come to a complete place of forgiveness and peace for themselves and maybe for those who hurt them, it's likely that for the majority, there's always something that we still hold onto. There certainly can be situations where we fully forgive all the people and painful episodes of our past wounds that allow us to move to a place where it becomes a positive vibration. However, I am more inclined to see this as a challenge that few will master until they completely detach from and release those deeply held feelings. It is the bad memory we keep consciously feeling or subconsciously remembering, as it lurks in our consciousness until we find another way of dealing with it. Or not. Forgiveness has benefits in the initial experience, but not if these memories continue to plague us in the future. Past wounds are important for us to resolve because we only hurt ourselves by hanging on to them. Our well-being matters. We allow our suffering as though it's a better choice than the truth, or because dogma tells us it is noble to suffer. Why?

As an alternative, I recommend moving to an authentically driven life which instead, allows us to live in a place of gratitude. This is another example of how we grow and develop as human beings. The movement of transcending to gratitude concerning how we view our past is where we find the-potential to bring us feelings of Love, contentment, and joy. These are some of the highest vibrations of all in manifesting what we wish for in life, which helps us in healing our abundance. The more time spent in these higher vibrations allows us to move to even higher realms of frequency. Moving to this stage means forgiveness is unnecessary.

"Forgiveness becomes a useful memory of what was, but is no longer useful."

When we can move to a place where we understand that everything arises out of Love, then the only thing we can do is to say thank you and be grateful for it all. Gratitude opens us up to feeling worthy of Love, but also of the full abundance we seek for ourselves without the limitations the ego mind brings.

Practicing gratitude, not just as an act of being polite, but from a place where we use it to acknowledge another person's self-worth, is important in our quest to heal ourselves and others. I read a fascinating article written by Dr. Kim Blackham, *The Three Levels of Gratitude*. She points out that gratitude at the first level, can be characterized as a way of being cordial to each other. For example, waving to another driver who let us cut in front of them while in bumper-to-bumper traffic or a thank you to our waitress for refilling our cup of coffee.

On the second level, we offer thanks and gratitude to those around us where we recognize the gift of who they are. We acknowledge their worthiness and their contribution to our lives through our being grateful to them. An example might be our child's 5th-grade teacher, where we send them a little gift of appreciation so that they feel how important they are to us. At this level, Dr. Blackham sees this not just as an expression of our thanks, but where it's an attitude that shapes our behavior. She beautifully goes on to say how it changes us to become aware and to acknowledge another person's worth. Essentially, an awareness of another person's contributions to our lives and the lives we hold dear around us. This is the place where gratitude helps to heal our past wounds and the beginnings of living in authenticity and on purpose. It helps us see our ability to use our positive feelings to connect with another human being and consequently, to attract the thing(s) we want in our life.

Offering gratitude on the second level is important for us to embody, as it allows us to let others know how valuable they are to us and the whole of humanity. Most of us have no problem doing so if someone does something nice for us, but it's the acceptance of gratitude that is most impactful to them and more meaningful when we give freely. Feeling their self-worth helps them to heal their self-inflicted wounds. When we allow it to have the same impact on us, is when we reach the third level that Dr. Blackman speaks of. I believe this may be the most difficult level to attain, but the most beneficial in our entire soul journey.

> *"It is on the deepest level of gratitude where we see ourselves as worthy enough to give ourselves permission to be loved."*

This is the key - to permit ourselves to be loved by others and most importantly, by ourselves. Here is where self-love emerges to heal our past wounds, so we can detach from relying on our ego to run our lives. It is the ego that is always seeking validation from other people and things outside of us. Instead, it helps us to understand our self-worth and the value that we bring to the world. This one-point sums up how we manifest anything in this world. What we give away, comes back to us tenfold. So, the gratitude we generously give to others expands their worthiness and helps us to truly feel worthy enough to be loved and BE Love.

"If you wish to receive more gratitude in your life, then give it away freely to others."

Why is this so important? Because seeing how much we contribute to the world enlarges what we feel we are worth receiving. Ken Honda describes this as "enlarging our money container," be it happiness, more money, or other forms of abundance. Many of us live with small containers, either subconsciously, or consciously, where we restrict the amount of abundance that could flow to us. So, worthiness is tied directly to healing our abundance and is a critical factor.

The significance of gratitude is that we're able to see our value. More importantly, Love within and for ourselves, along with loving our journey, is where we fill up with so much Love that all we can do is turn around and share and express that Love with others. This means to live our passion and do what we came here to do. It's also where gratitude becomes a part of us - it's Who We Are as we're choosing how to uniquely express ourselves. I can't overemphasize the importance of understanding that both gratitude and Love are two feelings that are crucial if we wish to manifest anything positive in our lives. So, it should come as no surprise that they are important emotions to make our dreams and wishes come true.

Start by loving ourselves and figuring out what beliefs we hold about experiences from our past that stop us. Decide that they are falsehoods we came to embrace for whatever reason. Then make it a personal quest to reach the third level of gratitude to help yourself feel worthy enough to accept praise or other forms of abundance in your life. Many of us have no problem with giving gifts to others but have a difficult time accepting them in return. We should be grateful both ways.

Let me share with you another experience I had about having a difficult time accepting gifts. This happened to me when I was in college. Friends of mine and I would often drop by a favorite restaurant for a meal or soft drinks and some happy talk, and we would always see one waitress who was a friend of my older brother. We were always generous to her in leaving a tip, but on one occasion, she told us not to worry as she would pick up the entire tab. Not wanting her to use her hard-earned money, we ended up leaving the cost of the meal and a big tip on top of that. She later confronted me and asked me why we did what we did. It was only until later that I realized I was denying her the ability to gift me and my friends. Worst of all, it made me realize I had a problem, I had a difficult time receiving anything - even compliments were embarrassingly accepted with some level of guilt and shyness, still a residual feeling of wanting to be small. If we keep refusing nice things that people do for us or want to give us, then how can we manifest even more abundance and money when it is offered to us, and we feel guilty or undeserving of accepting it? I didn't feel worthy enough at that stage to receive anything out of the Love I had for myself because I had very little Love inside. If we don't feel worthy enough to receive, we end up sabotaging our progress along the way and keep wondering why we never arrive.

Many people believe they don't deserve what they wish for because they either haven't worked hard enough or don't measure up to others doing things they wish they could do. This idea of "imposter syndrome" is being worried they don't have the credentials nor certificates to be called an "expert." As far as I'm concerned, if the message doesn't resonate with you, then find something and someone that does.

By withholding Who We Are, why make the journey in the first place? Regardless of what our experience was in the past, even if it was hitting rock bottom in despair if it finally allows us to be able to help someone else with the same problem, that is all that matters. The pathway to feeling "not good enough" eventually takes us nowhere except to a life unfulfilled, unhappy, and unfortunate.

Most of us have trouble receiving, which restricts the flow of abundance, due to our self-worth and how much we feel we deserve. Moving ourselves into that third level of gratitude is one of the final steps in getting past the limitations we've created for ourselves in our lives. This is where it becomes a part of us, of who we are, and who we wish to express and share with others.

Sarah McCrum, author of *Love Money, Money Loves You* has a wonderful exercise in her book asking the reader to discover how much they contribute to the world. One of the key aspects of this is that it forces us to review our life where we appreciate ourselves. In effect, raising our self-esteem and Love for ourselves.

This is an extremely important goal. So I would suggest making a daily list as she suggests, but instead asking the question, "What have I done in the past that I'm proud of having accomplished or successfully overcome"?

The purpose of this exercise helps us to memorialize all of the great deeds we've performed over the years and huge challenges we conquered along the way. We forget how courageous or how much we've grown as the result of those past events. We realize that even disappointments can be a source of great achievement. Remember we have the power to reframe anything in our lives in an effort to bring a higher self-esteem and expanded worthiness to ourselves. By doing so, it wonderfully addresses healing our relationship with money and everything else we wish for in the world.

To do this exercise, write down one experience you've had that you feel proud of. It doesn't have to be something big but should leave you with a sense of pride. On the following day, do the same thing, but before you do, read through all of the previous day's entries. You can imagine how empowering this exercise is in helping us boost our self-worth, self-confidence, and self-love, especially after ten months or a full year of practicing this habit.

Speaking from a personal basis, this exercise helped accelerate my life in so many ways, getting me into *Flow*, which will be covered in Chapter 11. The right people started showing up as well as resources. It was like the door had opened to synchronicity we often hear about.

So, my question for you to ask yourself is, "How do I matter in this world?" It's a reminder that we all do. This exercise reveals the contributions we've made and how positive an influence we've been to others. This is not about feeding our ego. Rather, it moves us away from it by elevating ourselves to a higher vibrational reality so things from our past no longer sabotage our success.

The more positive energy we put out into the world, the more of that positive energy is reflected in creating what we desire. It is the elevation of our inner worthiness that is key to feeling we deserve these big dreams and aid in the manifestation process. This is why it's important to regularly practice sharing sincere gratitude to others. The more you give out, the more you get back.

When I lived in Los Angeles, I was visiting my local McDonalds when a homeless guy approached me asking for money. I told him while I wouldn't give him any money, I would buy him anything he wanted if he was hungry. He happily accepted, but when I asked him what he wanted, he couldn't answer right away. After what seemed like forever, he embarrassingly asked for a regular hamburger and a small drink. I ended up buying him a supersize of everything and when I handed him the food, he lowered his head and thanked me in a soft tone of discomfort. When I got back to my car, I broke down and cried having witnessed that. I had offered this man anything he wanted on the menu and all he was able to ask for was the smallest size hamburger and the smallest size drink. At that moment, I wondered how one's self-esteem and self-worth could drop so low to settle for so much less. This man's feeling of worthiness for himself had dropped so low that his money container had shrunk down to something very tiny. Likewise, his emotional vibrations were also at a low point of feeling ashamed, which is at the bottom of the frequency range. How was he to manifest anything at that low energy, but more of the same hardship and poverty?

Worthiness is a necessary component of expanding our abundance and moving forward with our life. If you find yourself procrastinating and having a difficult time doing something you know benefits you, it could be that you don't feel worthy enough for the success that it'll bring. Or it could be your ego getting itself involved believing the bumpy road ahead is bad, when in reality it actually benefits us. We'll discuss procrastination and moving forward in an upcoming chapter.

When we receive gratitude at the third level, as Dr. Blackham notes, it gives us permission to be Loved. And with that, we feel worthy enough for all of the good things we want for ourselves. I don't know if this can be overstated; I have repeatedly stated that the whole reason why we are here is to help expand the Universe and we do that by coming here to experience and express Love in all of its depth.

I'm curious, to what extent was hugging done in your family while growing up? For me in Hawaii, hugging and "showing aloha" (love) is important among friends and families. Not all cultures use this type of expression. Certainly, hugging is not appropriate for all situations, but there is such a power in it. I admit it wasn't until my adult years that I learned of its power to transform and heal. I have been in situations of meeting people in such despair that a hug changes them instantly. Maybe it reminds us of the loving comfort our parents gave us. What's tragic is there are many cultures that stop showing physical affection to their children after reaching a certain age or not at all. In many workshops I've attended, I've hugged someone that I thought needed it and it changed them profoundly.

Hugging is "physical gratitude" and as covered earlier, makes a person feel worthy enough to be loved. Loved by others and eventually by themselves. This is the first step in experiencing Love and why we come here in the first place. Worthiness brings self-esteem and self-worth. which enlarges what we want for ourselves. Better yet, what we demand for ourselves.

"The power of Love
we express into the world to each other
has the power to give us everything we wish for in life."

The more significant our experiences are, the more significant our ability to express a passion that will touch other people's lives. But it's important to come to a place where we Love ourselves enough to see all our past mistakes and bad actions as "helpful." For me, it was those days and months I was homeless, living in a car that provided an opportunity to discover a Love for myself. For my friend, it was his drinking that almost killed him and caused him to lose his family and almost everything else. For some of you, perhaps you've had someone die unexpectedly, sending you into deep sorrow. Having come through all of that, the goal is to use those tragedies and bitter days and nights to find our unique gift that can help others. People that are suffering with the same challenges that we experienced but having a difficult time emerging from that dark part of their lives into the light of a new day. As in the law of opposites, we experience "unworthiness" to understand and embrace "worthiness."

CHAPTER SEVEN QUESTIONS

Take a few minutes to consider each question before answering in your journal. Write as much as you're inspired to. Review later after reading the entire book to see if your answers have changed in any significant way.

- Looking back to the past, think of someone who caused you great pain that was difficult to let go of. Have you fully forgiven that situation, or would you honestly say you put it out of your mind so you can get on with your life? Are there still some lingering negative feelings? How would you feel if you realized that person was there to help make you a better and stronger person?
- How important do you think gratitude is in expanding and healing our abundance? What level of gratitude do you think you're expressing right now?
- Based on what you have read about worthiness, how large do you believe your money container is and what can you do to expand its size?

- Ponder and answer this question over the next couple of days. "Why do I matter in this world?"

CHAPTER EIGHT
MONEY

Isn't it ironic that in this world of illusion, we have problems creating something that is an illusion? That is really at the heart of it all. To live in this world of illusion, we must play this game of illusion to create "illusionary" wealth, "illusionary" abundance, and anything else that matters to us. But the way to play the game of illusion is to decide NOT to play it. What I mean by this, is to not play by the rules of what the physical world is saying to us. Having all come from Source, we are so used to everything being created instantly. But here in this physical world of separateness and contrast, it's not as easy. For this, we use the Law of Attraction, the Law of Assumption, and Vibrational Manifestation to help bring us what we desire.

There are so many paradoxical things in this physical universe that offer a key to understanding how to use them to our advantage. They include the illusions of this world including time and space, the illusion of what's important, the illusion of limitations and the illusions of wealth and poverty. All of them help us maneuver through this temporary journey we're on. It is a subtle balance between using physical effort and harnessing the powers of our emotional vibrations to bring us to what we want. To help us function in this physical universe, we must avoid being overwhelmed by things that only appear real. As previously discussed, all things, whether we can see them or not, are vibrating particles with varying frequencies. This includes our emotions and thoughts, so through altering our emotional vibration, we align with that which we seek, as in the case of money.

Most of our deepest feelings of how we perceive money has everything to do with what we believe about ourselves and our worthiness. Being worthy enough for Love is the same as saying we are worthy enough to bless ourselves with personal abundance of all kinds.

It's always a choice as to how we view money as something evil to avoid and never befriend, or something helpful we want to establish a long-term positive relationship with. Some people believe life is about working hard and struggling as a measure of how they're doing. This external "ego" choice. It's important we evaluate our relationship with money and work towards befriending it rather than it being a stranger to us.

The reason why we have so much difficulty with money is that we've attached so many different meanings to it, most likely from our past or our parents. Therefore, there's no one particular way of resolving our situation since the meaning was formed in different ways for each of us. Money is something that assists us in creating things and is the reason why we feel we need it. But it's like all other things that we can manifest if we understand vibrational attraction, and how to approach all challenges in life. I speak of seeing money for what it truly is.

"Most of us believe money and wealth is like a pie in that there's only so many pieces to go around when in reality, it is limitless."

Money is vibration like everything in this Universe, so it's a matter of discovering that matching energy frequency to bring it to us. In no way are there limits on its creation and availability. Let's take what we learned about vibration and expand it here.

We know everything is some sort of vibration, even the things we cannot see like emotions. Yet it is these invisible feelings when used to visualize something we want, that help us to bring about the results we are looking for. All that is further required is for us to detach from it at some point and then take physical action when the opportunity presents itself. So true is the saying, "It's not being in the right place at the right time, but rather being in the right place at the right time - and knowing it!"

Everything in the Universe, including the earth and the sky, our homes and clothes, our paper money, and bars of gold, to our spectrum of emotions, all have a specific vibrating frequency. Yet the majority of us refuse to believe this fact because we evaluate things through our eyes and senses, which tells us that a chair, for example, is not the same as our car or for that matter, ourselves. This is the illusion of this world of separation we live in.

In truth, science has already proven that all matter in the universe is made up of tiny particles, as we previously discussed. The only difference is that everything is vibrating at different rates of speed. This is the reality we live in - although we insist on using only our physical effort to create what we want. We are all creating things using our emotions, it's just that we are unaware of this, and credit the results entirely due to our physical actions that brought it about.

The life you live right now is a result of you manifesting it based on the vibration of what you feel you deserve. This is what I describe as vibrational and invisible creation, living in a world in which we believe ourselves to be solid matter, physical bodies seemingly working independently with no connection to each other.

The "Schwinger effect," a scientific theory of Julian Schwinger, a Nobel Prize-winning physicist in quantum electrodynamics states that matter can be created from nothing, provided a particular electrical charge is applied. As with everything in the Universe, electricity is also vibrational energy. The ultimate goal here is for us to learn how to use our vibrational emotions for our benefit, rather than letting them create what we don't want. The tools we were given here to create with that bring us the things we want, are the same tools that bring us the things we fear the most. It is that delicate balance between applying spiritual intention and exerting physical action (both of which are vibrational), that brings to us what we want to manifest.

> *"The Universe and God are not conspiring*
> *against us to make things difficult.*
> *It only brings us what we think and feel."*

It's important to keep in mind that money in its physical state is still about circulation and a free flow of exchange, or rather the "velocity" of money to put it in another way. From a spiritual perspective, this is essentially increasing the energy flow to create more energy in return. Unfortunately, the way governments regulate money throughout the world creates a system of rewarding our hoarding of money, rather than spending and circulating it. In return, we earn a small amount of interest on our savings and investments, while the institutions are given freer access to our wealth to use it for themselves. The government oversees this speed and availability, using things like "quantitative easing" as a solution to providing more money to circulate to allow more liquidity. It is much more complex than this, which is why we have so much fear and anxiety around this topic when we don't understand something that we feel controls our entire lives. Our fears of the lack of money have us hold back on spending in times of a recession or impending recession. The problem is exacerbated by our feelings of lack and fear of not having enough, or other such things from our past. Not good when we want to stay in positive vibrational energy to help us manifest abundance.

Interestingly, Silvio Gesell, and 1890s economist came up with a theory of "expiring money" where money was issued with an expiration date. The only way of keeping it from expiring was to pay a small tax to affix a stamp to it. Later in 1932, the Austrian town of Wörgl did the same thing by issuing banknotes that would automatically lose 1% of their value each month. They hoped to bring their town out of a depression that affected the entire Western industrialized world and lasted a full decade starting in 1929. The result of this experiment was an amazing success, as people were forced to spend the money as quickly as they could to avoid the depreciation of their spending power. People were motivated to purchase groceries and services, to which the merchants did the same, and hire more staff where they would now earn a wage. Unfortunately, the Austrian government halted that practice a year later to regain control of the monetary supply.

While there are various ways to implement such a currency, especially as a digital one, the free exchange of money or the velocity of money is a great example of money "manifestation" from a spiritual energy exchange point-of-view. The Universe sees energy going out, so energy must return in some form and in some way, but not necessarily from the same source.

Remember us discussing earlier the law of opposites and appreciating the contrast? It's important to see money from that same point of view. At the beginning of this chapter, I remarked how ironic it is to live in this world of illusion and its importance to play the game of illusion to create illusionary wealth, abundance, and anything else that matters to us. This game I speak of is to see money, like everything else in this world, as having both a yin and yang side to it. In doing so, we realize its ability to create a contextual comparison for us to choose to either be enslaved by it or be empowered by it. Do we see it as friend or foe? Neither way is good nor bad, as it's dependent on how we wish to live our life this time around.

Keep in mind, that there are two sides to the creation of money and other things we want in our lives. Either we come from a place of the ego or one driven by authenticity and passion. Money vibration in ego sets us apart from it, whereas, in Spirit, we see everything as connected and no longer distant and unattainable. In using our ego and looking to nothing else but ourselves for solutions, many of us will do the things our parents and society told us to do - using money and/or prestige as the sole determinate of what job or occupation we decide upon, even though our heart is telling us otherwise. And then we move through life using external cues to make sure we're doing okay. Enough is usually never enough as we seek higher and higher reflections of these faulty external cues, so we are never happy, constantly looking for more. Creating money and happiness comes from us internally, so it's best to stop searching for money from outside ourselves.

Perhaps money was created as a contrasting dynamic that was meant to help us experience that choice like all these other contrasts. Maybe not intentionally, but it certainly is available to us now that we've placed so much importance on it. Money and the wide range of emotions that are created surrounding it, represent both opportunities and consequences to us. It is seen by most of us as the primary physical tool or medium to which we can bring almost anything or any situation we want, be it buying a new home, or car, or creating a successful company. But since we live in separation, we often focus on the gap - believing it's harder to obtain the things we want when it is not. An example many fall into is waiting in fear to deal with a bad financial situation while it just gets worse. We become anxious over it, and it repeats itself cycling downward. I have been there many a time to the dismay and disappointment of friends and family, but now use this experience to empower me to act.

Like all things with contrast, we develop mixed feelings about money like a love/hate relationship. Most of us have been conditioned to believe that God and Spirituality have no use for money, but we should remember that everything originates from Source. Money, like everything else, maybe even more so, sets up this contextual field of contrasts for us to make choices in our life in how we see it. What kind of feelings do you get when you think about having enough money to make you feel abundant? Do you see it as a friend or enemy? Is it something far off, distant, and difficult to create, or at your beck and call always there for you? Does it bring up feelings of fear and anxiety or joy and happiness? Interestingly, some people end up becoming wealthy and view money as a curse and a necessary evil.

So, it is very beneficial to remember the law of opposites, particularly when we're faced with some sort of hardship or challenge like the rent being due in two weeks when we've run out of options. The more we let this affect us and bring us down emotionally, the longer it will take for solutions to arrive. If we focus entirely on the worst-case scenario which expresses itself as fear and anxiety in our bodies, an even worse situation might arise, just because of the negative pictures and feelings inside of us. It's important to flip the negative emotions and see them as a positive thing, or at least try to see this as a non-event to keep us moving towards a higher vibration. The idea is to let the event come in and go out without emotion. Everything can be seen in a different light as it is happening to us - it's always a choice. As difficult as it may seem, the quicker we can move from negative emotions to positive ones, the faster we can move through it.

The law of opposites tells us we have a choice of how to react and it's important to remember that neither is wrong. Both serve us. This was covered previously,so go back and review it if need be.

We must never forget this part of us that is always of Source God. We have never been lost and we have always been there. We have just forgotten what we agreed to when coming here. And that is our ability to manifest things using our "vibrational intention, attention, and no tension," as Janet Attwood says in her life-changing Passion Test course. Following a life based on what we love to do helps to keep us in a positive emotional state more often than not. This makes manifestation easier - bringing us the things we want in life.

For many of us, this difficult relationship with money may have started when we were only children, influenced by our parents or grandparents. By acknowledging those past wounds and sincerely working to heal them, we can move to a place where the manifestation process is not sabotaged by the chains of our past.

For myself, my difficult relationship with money began because I misinterpreted my father's modesty about his success, leading me to feel embarrassed about our middle-class lifestyle. At that age, it was a time when I desperately wanted to fit in, lest I be ostracized at school, but the effects carried way into adulthood, unbeknownst to me. I can now see that, like many of you, I realized that our whole lives are in some way tied to having, receiving, or creating this thing called "money." Unfortunately, we all end up placing money on a pedestal as the controller of all things.

After a few unpleasant experiences, mixed in with some extremely good times, I found myself unable to deal with it all and ended up on the streets - homeless, for ten months. I distinctly remember that first night as I walked the streets, not knowing where to go and how to get myself out of this situation, sad, depressed, and embarrassed. How was I to move to a place of positive energy? No, it wasn't going to happen. Not that night at least, and not for months.

I was lucky to have a good friend loan me a car she wasn't using to live in while I bathed in cold showers down at the beach park. The 24-hour supermarkets and restaurants were a godsend as I could camp out and feel safe, but the thought was always whether some security guard or employee would get wise and knock on the window and ask me to leave. I didn't want to drive around at night using gas and the possibility of being pulled over by the police for something. As for eating, thankfully, there were-food stamps, which I got off of as soon as I was able. Food stamps, coupled with 7-11, was where I could buy cold prepared foods and heat them in their microwave. My favorite though was the cheap ramen which provided a hot meal with soup. With no home or kitchen, purchasing most of the other foods at the grocery store was impossible with no means to cook it or refrigerate it. Thankfully I was never a drinker or smoker, so I never had to deal with those issues.

I still remember the hurt of feeling so broken and lost. My self-esteem was at the bottom of the barrel, and it reminded me of the homeless man I had met at McDonalds that I mentioned earlier. Little did I know I would find myself in a similar position of being homeless years later and in the town I grew up in. I knew exactly how that man felt, feeling sorry for myself and a failure. Fortunately, that experience made me quickly realize the importance of staying positive, keeping a high self-worth and making the decision that whatever happens, I had to find a way out of this.

It wasn't until later that I began studying about emotions and vibrational frequencies. Only then did I come to understand it's almost impossible to move from a place of guilt and shame to happiness and abundance in one leap. When I was at my lowest point, it was necessary to inch my way out of this hole I was in, rather than expecting to leapfrog out. Although there might be rare exceptions, it's difficult to jump from those low negative feelings to very positive ones, especially when you've been living that way for awhile. Rather, we move within a range to reach a less negative emotion one at a time, to feeling alright with ourselves before anything positive is reached. All along, the negative low-vibrating emotions we experience keep us down, often bringing to us more things to depress us.

I'm not sure if most people are aware that for someone homeless with no address or phone number, it's almost impossible to get a regular job. Compounded by the emotional bleakness of the situation, it's rough unless someone has the strength to make the vibrational shift.

*"I had to give up and surrender
to the person I had become
in order to change
to the person who I really was."*

Remember that in the manifesting process, the idea of surrender is important to move onto the next step we wish for. In my case, it was to reject and surrender to the notion of what my current state was, based on how I saw my present circumstances, and instead, believe I could live in an entirely different and better reality. Remember the importance of getting rid or making space for things in our life in order for something new and better to appear. I now understood the meaning of, "this too shall pass" and it would all be-over one day. Certainly not with the mindset of winning the lottery, but just having a roof over my head was the big dream.

When I was homeless, I had very little energy to send out so how was I expected to receive any money energy in return? The important realization I made since that time was: if we attract what we want by how much positive energy we put out to the world, at that stage of my life, being homeless, how could I expect anything to change? In other words, my contribution to the world of positive energy was non-existent at that low point, so how could I expect anything of value and substance in return? This became abundantly clear when I did Sarah McCrum's daily exercise of writing down what we're proud of, as a way for us to see how much value we contribute to the world. It is an uphill climb when one sinks to that level as it normally takes time to shift our emotions.

It was a good experience though in looking back as it taught me a whole lot about myself, my strengths, the friendships, the people who cared about me, and to continue my passion for studying life, and yes, even putting it in print to share with you now. It helped me understand the importance for all of us to feel worthy enough to receive. While my experience may have not been as severe as some others, the guilt and shame that accompanied it, I'm sure is almost universal. And now knowing those two emotions are at the bottom of the frequency vibrational range, it makes me wonder how I recovered from it.

Perhaps what has been the biggest takeaway from all of this is the importance of not only how worthy we need to feel, but also understanding how much we actually contribute to the world. Realize that it'll never happen externally - it must happen internally, starting with us loving ourselves. To reiterate, the deepest level of gratitude is one where we give permission to ourselves to be worthy and loved. If I were in that situation again, I would give away as much gratitude to other people I could because that is what I would receive in return. That is what will boost my ability to increase the size of my tiny money container. Until we can truly love ourselves, it's difficult to attract vibrationally any of the things we feel we deserve to have during this lifetime.

We must keep reminding ourselves that money is just another illusion and that it serves a purpose. It teaches us how to deal with need and lack in a constructive vibrational way. The emotions and vibrations emanating from the feelings of lack and need for money is understandable. But it's also detrimental knowing that to successfully manifest what we want; we must match the positive vibration of it. Lack and need is at the bottom of the frequency spectrum.

My long-held falsehoods about being ashamed of money got me there and wouldn't get me out until I dropped the shame. I had to realize those were the misunderstandings of a child that didn't know better.

It kept me struggling for years, despite making a lot of money at different times in my life. Once I removed the stigma I felt about money, everything changed.

Like Love, happiness, and many other things that we feel separated from, money is also included on that list. In truth, there is unlimited abundance of every kind that the God Source is. This discussion is useful in our experiencing and understanding how to manifest money despite these self-imposed limitations. Money is another illusionary "thing" we feel we need for a variety of reasons. It is the ego that creates the separation between us and what we desire, feeling that it's beyond our reach and control to obtain it.

Beyond basic needs, the ego perpetuates the desire for more - to owning a nicer car or having a higher salary than our co-worker. Whether it arises out of the desire to be better than others or just as a way of feeling secure, the all-out attachment to it does not make manifesting it any easier. The only answer is to live the life that brings us the most joy, by expressing our real self or real you.

The whole notion of how we see money needs to change. It is not something to be afraid of, to avoid, or to have disdain for, but rather seen as a friend who wants us to be happy in our lives. As Ken Honda says, "When money leaves your house, thank it for spending time with you and invite it to return with more friends." So, make it a point to get to know it and befriend it. In my conversation with money, I was surprised, because its first response was to ask me, "Why are you so afraid of me?"

CHAPTER EIGHT QUESTIONS

Take a few minutes to consider each question before answering in your journal. Write as much as you're inspired to. Review later after reading the entire book to see if your answers have changed in any significant way.

- How have your parents and others from your past influenced your beliefs about money? Can you identify exactly where it came from?
- Would you say you feel enslaved by money or empowered by it? Explain why.
- What kind of relationship do you currently have with money? Would you say you feel enslaved by it or empowered? Is it a friend that loves being around you or a foe, who you fight with all the time? Take your time with answering these questions. You might consider having a conversation with money as covered in the book.
- How much positive money energy do you put out into the world? Make a list of things you've accomplished that has brought value to society and to yourself.

CHAPTER NINE

MANIFESTATION AND SELF-SABOTAGE

Like many things in this dualistic and illusional world of form, life is filled with so many contradictions. Death is not the permanent end we've come to believe but rather a transformation from form to formless. What we perceive of Love and happiness being "somewhere out there" that we somehow lack and need to go looking for is a fallacy. They exist entirely inside of us and once we recognize it is, only then does it show up externally. But keep in mind that if we believe ourselves to be incomplete, then an incomplete person will show up for us. Manifestation uses the vibrational energy of how we see ourselves to bring us a match to who we are and not what we want. I'm not sure who to credit for this insightful quote and I might be paraphrasing, but it's profound.

> *"You don't manifest what you want,*
> *rather you manifest who you are."*
> *—Unknown author*

The creation of anything we believe we lack in ourselves can only bring us more lack. Abundance arrives when we feel abundant, not one second sooner. Despite countless claims of bringing what we wish for instantly, there are so many details important in this process. This chapter covers a discussion of how to bring those things we desire into our lives and what might keep us from reaching them. Namely procrastination and self-sabotage.

Governing everything are the Law of Attraction and the Law of Assumption. Like everything else in the Universe, aligning our vibrational frequency is the key. What complicates matters however, are our numerous past wounds and tribal customs we grew up with. All of them serve to either hinder or help us to succeed. Hinder by procrastinating or sabotaging ourselves because we believe we're not good enough. Or helping in making us feel more courageous through overcoming these contrasting experiences.

It is the ego reinforced by the unpredictability of the subconscious mind that keeps us from realizing the truth of the infinite power we possess. Having come from the God Source, we ARE everything that God is and missing nothing. But living this illusional existence feeling alone and separated keeps us from knowing and believing our own true greatness. So we use procrastination and self-sabotage to help us confirm our ineptness and loneliness.

Most experts would define procrastination as putting off something we see as threatening but feel a necessity to do. It has nothing to do with being lazy as in fact, most procrastinators actually have an overt sense of responsibility. Perhaps it is us having such high expectations that we don't think we can measure up to what others might expect of us.

Self-sabotage is quite similar to procrastination with regards to stopping us from accomplishing things we know will benefit us. However, it also includes situations where we take action in a detrimental way resulting in quite the same unwelcomed results. Both offer us the opportunity to challenge us to become better people or keep us on a treadmill of constant disappointment.

This constant worry of how we are perceived by others is as you've come to understand, choosing to live through our ego. Procrastination and self-sabotage are tools to help the ego protect us. We fill ourselves with questions doubting our abilities. What happens if I do accomplish this task and I become very successful? Will people still like me anymore or will they take advantage of me? Do I have what it takes to be this new person?

And yet in this world of contradictions, both hinderances can serve as both a benefit and detriment to our experience. It is up to us to decide through free will on whether we wish to have it empower us or disable us. This is all part of the human experience. We can see it helps us in the development of our perseverance and courage when breaking through. Everything has a dualistic nature to itself.

Before we go further, let's review some key points important to successfully creating the things we wish to manifest into our lives. Ignoring these issues delay or make it difficult to bring us what we desire in life.

- Like a radio or television, we bring to us the "channel" we wish for. So, if it's positive abundance we desire, we must shift our vibrational energy to match it. Tune to the exact frequency or in other words, gain a clear and concise idea of what it looks and feels like. More importantly is how we feel and act when we have stepped into the who that we are.

- Being in the state of lack will only bring us the same. We cannot wish for things to change except to change our identity first.
- Work to resolve as many past wounds as possible and view these adversities as positive gifts because without doing so, our egos may sabotage ourselves subconsciously as a way of protecting us.
- The ego is always in the process of protection against what it perceives to be detrimental to our wellbeing. This could lead us to a misunderstanding of whether the actions we are taking are derived out of true Love or from the ego.
- Being good to ourselves in the present moment is critical, which is why resolving past wounds is helpful.
- A good practice is to make a list of all the good things happening in our life and

review it daily. If you can't think of anything, search your memory until you find some.
- You will never find true abundance until you feel worthy enough to accept it into your life.
- Understand that everything in this Universe, including money, is Love and so anything having to do with Love is important in the manifestation process. Hence the critical role of loving ourselves.
- Move from a place of ego where the focus is on things external to us, to one of authenticity where we look internally for answers. By doing so, it insulates us from people and situations that have no bearing on our worth and our journey here.

Insisting on living through this false lens of the ego will steer us in the direction where our dreams and goals are fleeting and empty. It will offer temporary gratification, but soon it will cause us to seek for more empty goals. Recognize that even comparing our present self to a "better" one in the future is an endless quest for more. There will come a time when one must realize pushing ourselves to "make more" is but an empty shell of a life with no real purpose. That is of course, unless your intention for this lifetime is to experience this type of existence. One of continually needing more validation of your self-worth through external examples.

What exactly is the manifestation process? Simply put, it is the act of continually focusing our thoughts, emotions, and feelings on what we desire in our lives in a very realistic way until it becomes Who We Are. The brain doesn't know the difference between something we've imagined and feel so vividly, and something we've done physically. Yet it goes beyond just the visualizations and a shift of our emotions and feelings. It means to come to a place where we embody our "future" identity and how we see ourselves.

The term "future" is a bit of a misnomer because time only exists for us in this realm of play acting we're currently experiencing. A more accurate way is to call this your "True Self of Being." The Course in Miracles says that the past and future are mere illusions to perpetuate this world of separation.

While very useful in providing the motivation to keep us experiencing things, time could also serve to hinder us. "Future" events are always seen as detached, implying certain things are needed to happen before we get what we desire. Whereas within Universal Consciousness, it is BEING it and embracing the Who That We Are that is key. Do you see the reason why being authentic and honest with ourselves rather than living through our ego is so important? Demanding to live authentically brings us the answers and results we wish for.

"Be not fooled of a future that never comes,
for it is right there beside us,
once we recognize it is really us".

Coming to an understanding of the paradoxical world we live in can be quite a challenge. Simply put, it's important we arrive at a place of knowing and being something before it ever happens. This is why so many fail at manifesting abundance because the inherent nature of wanting brings us only more wanting. In other words, being in lack only brings us more evidence of being without.

If all it takes is to assume this new identity, then taking on this new persona should be easy. The difficulty is creation is controlled by parts of our mind that we have limited access to. Furthermore, some of us are stuck in fear of inadequacy based on childhood experiences or inherent cultural beliefs. Most of us don't want to let go of our current selves. Self-doubt will manifest itself as procrastination and self-sabotage. This directly affects us if we learned as children that money is evil and poverty virtuous. If we unknowingly hold these false beliefs, then manifesting becomes much more difficult than to have our lives change as a result of positive thoughts.

So what are these parts of our mind to be aware of? Most professionals agree we have a conscious and subconscious (or unconscious) mind. Yet it's the metaphysical and spiritual realms that help us to understand the super conscious mind as well. All three influence how we perceive things, our behavior, how we think and act. For the sake of our discussions here, these are the definitions for each. Let me say upfront that not everyone will agree on these exact interpretations.

Often referred to as the "waking mind," the conscious mind is the one we believe oversees our normal decision-making and problem-solving. Hence, we think of it as being in control of what we do during our daily activities as to our actions, thoughts, and feelings. In reality, the conscious layer plays a small role in what decisions are actually made.

Using the conscious mind to provide meaningful and permanent change can be challenging. It involves identifying the false beliefs we hang onto that tend to be illusive. But once they are discovered, we can replace those negative ideas of who we are with new empowering ones. Some use techniques such as hypnosis and past life regression through other parts of the mind to enable meaningful change.

Whichever modality we choose however, it is our subconscious mind that does its best to steer us unknowingly back to what it believes to be safe harbor. Also known as the "unconscious mind," the subconscious mind is one that stands behind silently in full control of the decisions we make. Unconscious habits usually reside here. The subconscious mind is in truth the one overseeing most of our feelings and unconscious thoughts and behaviors.

As we grow up, it gets filled with experiences that influence the opportunities we either take or steer away from. Maybe it's some trauma of being bullied in school or sexually abused early on that stops us from expressing ourselves later in life. Or just the opposite where our past experience helps us to capitalize on situations most would shy away from. All of this is collectively stored here, often unbeknownst to us.

The subconscious mind is like our "auto pilot," willing to take us anywhere if it's programmed correctly. This is the challenge though. While the subconscious mind will accept most of the beliefs we impress upon it, gaining access to it is protected by the ego. These are usually feelings of fear or of not being good enough.

Some see the ego as acting like a filter between our conscious and subconscious minds. Having the sole duty to protect us, it ultimately keeps us from finding true bliss. It is that tiny voice inside us suggesting it's okay to procrastinate on something even if it eventually would lead us to complete abundance.

Lastly, there's the "superconscious" mind that many spiritual people and metaphysicians theorize to exist, which resides above all else. Here is what some call our "higher self" as a personal connection to God and Universal Knowledge. This is where I believe our intentions for this lifetime are stored. This is where "knowing" comes from. It is our inner compass, often accessible when we raise our vibrational level through meditation and gratitude. Here is where inspirational thought, beautiful music, higher level ideas and bliss reside.

Together, all three areas of the mind influence our actions and outcome in the manifestation process. This happens through our understanding the purpose each serves in our journey here. Whether we choose to allow our ego to influence us is up to us. The alternative is of course living with purpose and following our inner voice through the superconscious mind.

A deeper discussion of these inter-relationships of our mind are for another book. Here, we are focusing on the fundamentals of manifestation to bring forth that which we are. These basics include the Law of Attraction and the Law of Assumption. Both assist in our understanding of how to bring forth our desires through the use of vibrational energy exchange.

The Law of Attraction says that whatever energy we put out, whether positive or negative, will attract the same. Whereas the Law of Assumption uses as its starting point a belief that one has already acquired what they wished for. In other words, longing versus having. Both laws, along with manifestation, are simple to understand, but not necessarily easy to master.

These laws are always operating whether we like it or not. Physical manifestation is taking place continuously through our feelings, thoughts and actions. So whatever your current circumstances are, you created this based on what's inside of you. Hence the reason why the process for some will require them to do a lot of internal repair work beforehand. This is compounded because the ego will often give us a false sense of our self-worth making it difficult to understand who we really are.

> *"How can we discover what our truth is if the question is wrong?"*

We start the manifestation process by placing ourselves fully into the place where what we desire has already come true. The more real it is for us is the goal, as well as a complete and clear understanding of what that looks and feels like. What are your thoughts and concerns as this new person? A lack of clarity about what we desire is the fundamental obstacle to change along with how we feel.

The paradox of this world is being that which we desire before we actually are. So wishing and hoping to receive a large sum of money while broke will never happen. The two vibrations do not match. We must move into a reality of living as though it has already occurred.

Ask yourselves, what would my life look and feel like when I've reached that goal? What would I be doing consistently on a day-to-day basis living in such a way? What would I be thinking of? How would I be reacting to things and people as this new person? There is a profound difference when knowing money will never be an issue ever again in our lives.

Suspend the notion of a future self that you must work towards and instead think of this new person you wish to be sitting right next to you as your True Self of Being. Be absolutely crystal clear on what this new identity of yourself is. What are you thinking and feeling about life? How do you carry yourself when with other people? How do you believe you fit into this world? Now step into that new you with all your confidence and authenticity driven by the passion to help others.

Leave behind any semblance of the former self. This is your ego that has been keeping you at bay because it felt threatened at your forward progress. Thank it for helping get us this far and "walk away."

It should be visually and emotionally clear that this is your new reality. Making the move from complete poverty to wealthy will be challenging if it's too big of a leap. Since everything is a shift in vibrational energy, a jump from the shame and despair of poverty to the joy and bliss of complete wealth is highly unlikely. We must allow our worthiness to catch up with us. Unless we feel deserving and worthy, change is difficult.

Again, it's important to entirely become that identity and see it for who you are. Are you living authentically and congruent to what you wish to be? If you wish to live a wealthy lifestyle but still believe money is the root of all evil, it'll be impossible to change.

Work it to the point where you use your senses to feel that what you want has already happened. This means aligning our daily actions to the person we see ourselves to be, so true that we are living "as if." And when I say living "as if," it also means taking actual physical action when we see a mismatch in where we are to where we want to be. I am also speaking of taking the action of meditating, eating better, exercising, and other life-enhancing actions.

Having come from Source where manifestation is instantaneous, these physical actions are crucial while in the process. Just remember that our view of ourselves and how we value what we deserve to receive, is clouded and sometimes obscured by beliefs from the past through the lens of our ego, unfortunately.

So if you find you're procrastinating or sabotaging yourself or you're manifesting the wrong things into your life, then maybe taking a step back is wise. You may still have some past wounds to heal. This is why it's so important to expand our worthiness so we instinctively know we deserve more - an important point that can't be stressed enough in this process.

Without that burden, let's say for example that you want to manifest a lump sum of money to pay off all your credit card balances. How would you feel when you held that check in your hands? Would you call some close friends and share that excitement? If so, what would you say to them and how would they react? Imagine depositing a huge check into your bank account as you hand it to the teller with your deposit slip. Then when you get home, access your account online and view the balance in your account. Are you happy and what does that feel like? Are you relieved? Excited? Now picture yourself going to your online credit card account and instead of paying just the minimum monthly payment, you click on the box that says, "Pay full balance." Do you have a smile on your face while doing so? What's going through your head and body as you make that choice and hit the "OK" button? Move yourself forward in time when you check your credit score. If you've paid off all your balances, your score will go up. What is your reaction? Are you proud of yourself? Do you now plan to apply for more credit? See yourself receiving instant approvals when you apply and fully experience the feelings associated with that happening. Live this over and over again and repeat it as many times during the day as possible, as you are living as though it has already occurred.

One excellent way is what I call "crowd creation," although others may have described it differently. In this scenario, find a group of close friends who will act out aloud "as if." Arrange to meet for an hour each week where everyone creates their True Self of Being for themselves, agreeing not to "break character" at any time. Share experiences of what your True Self did last week and what you intend to accomplish for the next week.

The goal is to express our feelings about this new identity and to share and relive the emotional joy that supposedly occurred. For example, "Share with us in detail what it felt like when such-n-such happened and what was your reaction?" Then when the following week rolls around, continue the stories, but resist the temptation to speak about your present situation.

It takes some practice, and it may feel awkward at first, but soon you'll experience a rush of excitement with everyone living their new identities and everyone offering comments as though it's a reality now. You must become the actor in your own stage play described in the first chapter. If you're stuck in a job you hate and can't imagine a better life, then you won't get out. Plain and simple.

Remember, we don't manifest what we want, rather we manifest who we are, as the famous quote goes. And it's less about what we're asking for than the person we become. It is essentially who we believe and know we are inside, and until we align with that, little will manifest for us. Just repeating mantras will not get us there nor looking at a vision board without emotion - we must shift our identity.

*"It is less about the 'stuff' we wish for
in our manifestation process.
Rather, it is the resulting person we become
that's the key."*

It reminds me of many great actors who become their role because the character they portray becomes who they are. And if they are believable to the audience, their entire identity shifts where they believe it and we believe it.

I can't stress enough, that this is why moving from ego to living honestly within ourselves in authenticity is so important because we stop looking at things we wish for outside of us to give us validation. Don't confuse this with working to obtain a certain identity. Keep in mind that our identity is determined by how we value ourselves. Moving toward a false identity based on wanting others to be impressed by what we own or how much we earn, will only bring us a false sense of self and eventual unhappiness. It's so important for us to believe in ourselves and that we feel deserving of all that we wish for, possessing the self-worth of receiving abundance and Love.

While we've pointed out the importance of Love throughout this book, sometimes the ego will mislead us. This is a misunderstanding of what true love is for ourselves. It's the ego choosing things to give us immediate satisfaction to protect us from our deep-seated fears. Like giving in to eating junk food for immediate gratification versus following the long-term plan of healthy living.

How do we know when our actions arise out of true love or the ego? It is NOT true love when the ego is present. The ego says I'm doing this so we don't get hurt. Or the ego says we're doing this because we just want to feel good right now. As you move through this manifestation process, be vigilant of anything your subconscious mind is using to keep from making progress. Are you usually procrastinating believing it's in your best interest? Do you find ways to justify your actions telling yourself this is good for me when it actually isn't? Without paying attention, this can be a long process.

For us to believe we can have all these wonderful things takes gratitude, because gratitude helps us feel worthy enough to be Loved and receive everything else in the world we wish for. We must find the true Love that is always available to us inside if we choose to claim it.

The final component of the process of manifestation is the act of "letting go" and taking the appropriate physical action necessary. This is the point where there is nothing else left to do because we've arrived. It's the feeling of BEING. However, it may be one of the most difficult concepts to understand. Living under the illusion of time, it's hard to imagine just stepping into a future reality. Except that it is not a future persona of ourselves, but rather just another vibrational version of us. Our True Self of Being which we spoke of earlier.

Before we arrived from Source, we were complete and whole, but now as individuals, we experience the feelings of lack until we move ourselves back into this state of Being. There is nothing for us to learn, just remembering. There is no place we need to reach because we never left. It's the same feeling as studying for a test and getting to the point where we say to ourselves, "I know this." We've all been there before. It is the feeling of complete fulfillment, knowing "I AM THIS." It's that certainty of breaking out from the shell of uncertainty.

In reaching this point in our creation, we surrender and detach ourselves from the outcome and just allow it. We realize we're home, comfortable where we are internally, but feeling different in a new identity, maybe in a new-looking body. We are confident and at peace that everything coming to us can be no other way.

Surrendering is often very useful in the manifestation process if we find ourselves coming to the place of "wanting" and "needing." The act of surrendering is essentially letting go of expectations of what we're wishing for. In the Conversations with God cosmology, there is no need or wanting. We are all part of the wholeness of the God Consciousness so need is non-existent. By our very act of needing, it is telling the Universe we don't have it. Plus, wanting is also a futile expectation of something that will never happen. Both need and wanting infer we are in the state of lack. The Law of Attraction will then bring us more lack. The reason surrendering is the appropriate response is it allows us to detach from any expectations that arise out of the manifestation process.

Each of us experiences lack or inadequacies in different parts of our lives. It's up to us to embrace those lower vibrational beliefs about ourselves and make the shift into BEING for each of them.

Taking the appropriate physical action is important to complete the process. Sometimes we get so caught up in the non-doing part or where self-sabotage steps in. Maybe it's to accept that new position we wished for that is being offered to us. Or putting in an offer to buy that perfect home we envisioned that we've just found. This will be simple if we've worked through our demons. This is where we are already being in this new identity of ours. It's an obvious step so take it and enjoy it!

CHAPTER NINE QUESTIONS

Take a few minutes to consider each question before answering in your journal. Write as much as you're inspired to. Review later after reading the entire book to see if your answers have changed in any significant way.

- Write about a time in your life when you were certain that you had done all you could do to prepare for something. This is the act of *being* and surrendering to the outcome. How did you feel?
- Would you say you practice procrastination or self-sabotage on a daily or regular basis? Take stock in seeing if you constantly put off doing things or sabotage yourself at one particular moment in your progress. If so, it's important to find out what is the root cause. Make a list of things from your past that you believe is causing this apprehension. If necessary, dig a little deeper. Take as much time here as your responses could be profoundly revealing and helpful.

- Be crystal clear of this new identity you wish to embody. Then find a few forward-thinking friends and start a "crowd creation" group. Agree to meet at least once a week with everyone acting in their new identity and not "breaking character." Write down your observations here or in your journal and discuss within your group if you feel so inclined.
- How often do you find yourself in the state of wanting and needing? Practice surrendering and see what happens. Write about your experience.

CHAPTER TEN
AUTHENTICITY

Authenticity is our natural state of being God, while in this separated physical realm. It means living the real you that allows abundance to flow into our lives and what I call, the "art of living you." It is our true and honest self that knows what we came here to do. It is our guiding light to our soul's path that leads us to our ultimate destination - our own truth. This is what we are as a fully expressed human BEING, so rather than stressing over how to find and reach this place, just relax, and let it be. The more honest we are with ourselves, the more is revealed to us.

> *"Authenticity is our natural state of being as God while in this physical realm."*

As a reminder, our main purpose and what we're here for is to experience and express Love in its full nature and to have fun while we're here. There are an infinite number of ways for us to achieve this goal guided by our free will. If we choose to seek a way other than what our heart is whispering to us, that's fine, but we could find ourselves off course, and often frustrated and unhappy. That doesn't make it wrong if that is what we strongly feel is right for us. But I'm referring to being honest with ourselves and our true feelings about what makes us happy. Certain choices may seem right because we got the house, we got the car, and we got the job, but we're not happy. Perhaps we either made choices because we thought it was "the right thing to do," or because, our parents would be proud of us. But was it? Nagging questions within us keep popping up wondering if maybe there's something more to life and we should follow those urgings, something that has more meaning that calms the restlessness of our soul.

"It's like the feeling of being lonely in a room full of people."

Before this point, the ego has done well for us. It's kept us happy, but cracks appear on the surface if we're willing to seek answers deep inside ourselves - some from the present, but many from the past, where the ego has helped perpetuate untruths that we now live and are comforted by. This is about doing things we know in our hearts are not who we are. Are we holding a false image of ourselves because we're so bent on impressing others, or are we too embarrassed for others to see our true selves? We all have felt it sometime in our lives for whatever reason. That tiny inner voice advising us to either not do something or take a chance. No doubt, we'll often make the wrong choices, only to understand later what the right choices are. Don't be so hard on yourself; you did what you thought was right at the time. Besides, you have the right to change your mind. It may not necessarily be about some specific thing that alters our life, but the more we increase our vibrational energy, the more of these messages we'll receive to set us on the right path.

As for me, my journey was quite arduous as I was ruled by my ego when I wanted to do things that impressed others. You know, like many of us who work so hard to get all those letters after our name (MBA, PhD, MD) or job title (CEO, CFO, COO) or whatever. There is nothing wrong with getting those titles if they help us in defining our passion, turning it into a profession and allowing us to help others find their way. If it's mainly done to impress others, it's for a negative reason and that's not good.

So, despite my love for the creative arts and even enrolling as an art major in college when I first came out of high school, it was my after-school job that controlled my life. As I excelled, they gave me more and more responsibility which meant that I'd spend less and less time at school. At some point, however, I decided to return to study full-time and get a degree. However, this time I listened to my ego and "common sense," and changed my major to enroll in the business college at my university - and also to make my dad happy. Little did I know it was more about satisfying the ego than anything else. After graduating, I joined my father in business, but I hoped to move to New York City and work there as a Commercial Real Estate Investment Feasibility Analyst. Sounds impressive, right? Before getting there, I ended up opening my own business, which failed. Life was kind of boom and bust for me and I'm sorry to say I hurt some people during the bust times. Now I see that at that time, I had yet to love and embrace all ~~of~~ my past fears and insecurities which were the cause of my failures, mostly following my head instead of my heart.

A major turning point came when I moved to New York City; not in commercial real estate, but to work with a marketing and motivational seminar company. I remember reading author Dr. Wayne Dyer's book, *Real Magic*, just before leaving. It was instrumental in pushing me closer to what that inner voice was saying to me. After spending half a year moving from coast to coast and back, unsure of what I wanted to do, I finally settled in Los Angeles. There, my hunger for inspiration and spirituality widened and flourished as I found myself immersed in all the wisdom I could find to study, attending seminars with Dr. Wayne Dyer, and multi-day retreats in Ashland, Oregon with Neale Donald Walsch. This was shortly after his Book One of *Conversations with God* was published. Southern California was perfect because there was always something nearby to attend to further the growth of my soul.

The move to New York opened the door, but the relocation to Los Angeles changed me, as I put aside my big ego aspirations to instead pursue what interested me. Rather than some financial analyst with a nice blue suit, I traded that for jeans and a polo shirt as a "go-fer" messenger working at CBS Television Studios in Hollywood. It was an ego buster coming from an executive position to someone who was rarely acknowledged or seen when walking through the offices. However, that job proved pivotal to me because I made quite a few connections there. One in particular was a publicist for a famous movie star, which helped me secure my first celebrity interview.

The initial plan in moving to L.A. was to do a radio interview show. This was around the time the internet was just getting started and there was no such thing as social media, let alone YouTube. Video production shows were quite costly, so the alternative was radio. Think of it like a podcast streamed over radio waves instead of the internet.

The celebrity I had an interview with was Steve Allen, an old-time comedian, performer, author, and songwriter, who was extremely popular. Steve Allen was the very first host of the famed Tonight Show, made extremely popular by Johnny Carson and later hosted by Jay Leno, Conan O'Brien, and Jimmy Fallon. I was given 45 minutes for this audio interview with Allen, but we ended up chatting for over two hours. In the end, Allen complimented me on my interviewing skills and encouraged me to pursue that field. Looking back, it's interesting how one little comment from one particularly significant person can change the course of a person's life, as he did for me. Interviewing all types of people is what I love to do because it helps others to be inspired by their stories.

Unfortunately, it took me years to acquire enough courage to follow through with the gift he saw in me. I returned home a few years after that interview and the Death Valley vision quest. My parents were growing older, and I wanted to spend more time with them before they passed. It was then that I began to explore the subject of death and dying in hopes of better preparing myself for what I knew was inevitable.

Meanwhile, to support myself, I went back into Commercial Real Estate Financing. I still thought it would bring me the financial success to finally do what I loved to do. You know, the adage, "Once I make my millions, I can do whatever I want," ego mentality. Things were going quite well for the most part until I found myself on the opposite end of things, leaving me on the streets.

Ironically, or maybe not so much, it took having me lose it all before I decided to be honest with myself in terms of how I wanted to live the rest of my life as an author and storyteller. In retrospect, I had tasted what it was like in Los Angeles, but as soon as I returned home with family and friends, my ego convinced me the logical thing to do was to put aside what I felt was right, and instead do what brought me more prestige. The choice was clear to me, at the time I was controlled by my ego because all that mattered to me then was what other people thought of me, the title I had, and the money.

In retrospect, I see that was all part of the plan. When I began my journey, I chose the road less traveled but became fearful of what society might think. Having to take cold showers at the beach while I was homeless changed me quite a bit. I realized what I had gotten myself into, and it was embarrassing. Although I was careful to hide my predicament from friends, I suspect that some were aware and may have been whispering behind my back. I don't know as none of them came to me to offer help. At this point though, I feel liberated and free of my past and how I failed. It now gives me the strength and clarity of how to help others. I now know that honesty borne out of authenticity comes from how well we understand that it is more about being guided by our inner self, rather than this idea of acting on how we feel.

As for my interviews, the medium has changed since those days and my focus sharpened over the years knowing that we can learn from everyone. Those early days most certainly set the stage and gave me a taste of what I was yearning for. The trouble was that I had little courage to follow through with it at that time; I now have a YouTube channel where I've interviewed some amazing individuals.

To deal with this illusion of living in a world of separation, we use our ego to help us decide, maneuver, understand, and experience who we believe we are. We come to recognize what our abilities and limitations are, eventually making judgments of what's important to us. The problem is that the ego offers us a false sense of our real potential selves and comes from a place of fear. It sees limitations in everything, making life a struggle. We must figure out who we are to express that which we are.

My authentic self kept telling me to follow my heart and help others to get to know themselves. But it took me struggling, homeless, and eventually living in a car that smacked me across the face to tell me I was not headed in the right direction. In reality, I hated being in business and dealing with some of the types of people it brought to the table. I was only enamored with the idea of what others thought of me with my fancy business cards and title. It was a life completely driven by my ego, seeking to impress people and not at all what brought joy to my heart that would lead to expressing Who I Am.

I never imagined that keeping a daily journal would be the tool I would eventually use to share these principles with others. It all started some 30 years ago in Manhattan when I began writing my observations, experiences, thoughts, and inspirations into one of those black-and-white marbled composition books. I would discover later that somehow, the inspirations turned out to be a great deal of automatic writing episodes. Many of these inspirational thoughts came from what I believe to be the "God Source" because when I read them back later, I wondered where those epiphanies came from. Certainly not from the me that I saw in the mirror. I came to understand that my writing partner in all of this is an entity called "Diana." That was the name I heard as clear as a bell when I was living in Los Angeles one quiet night after being woken from sleep. I thought it might have come from someone outside my bedroom window that looked out into the next-door neighbor's driveway, but there was no one and the clarity of this voice was not coming from outside nor in a dream. It was like someone was whispering the name into my ear.

My journey in moving from ego to authenticity was not easy, and certainly not swift. Looking back, I was kicking and screaming all the way there, resisting the change that Diana was gently pushing me towards. I made quite a few detours, taking the roads less traveled, and often stopped at roadside distractions which in retrospect, were all wonderful experiences. I had too many fears wrapped up in me, nor could I admit I loved myself. Ending up homeless helped me to give up all my previous perceptions of trying to impress other people, and instead, dedicate myself to seeking the inner truth deep within me. It was Diana who eventually explained to me that resisting all those things from my past did no good if I was unable to take anything away from the experience. So rather than trying to discard the memories and feelings of the past, she encouraged me to embrace it and make it a part of who I am.

She also said that when our past becomes an integral part of us and is no longer something we are ashamed of, we make peace with it. Even though the past and future are but illusions that our ego has created for us, they are essential for our journey. Thank your ego for helping us experience the contrast that allows us to choose to speak our truth. It has been there to help us understand and discover that which is our authentic God self. Indeed, we often have to figure out what we don't want to understand what we do want. Think of it like removing an outer layer or a suit we have on, but it doesn't require us to create a new persona. Instead, we are only removing the suit to reveal our real self, our true self. The removal of that outer layer is revealing what has been there all along. Or if you prefer, to that True Self of Being sitting next to us that we can simply step into.

However we see our true inner selves, they do not form as we are growing up. Rather, it is and always has been us as Who We Are. The part that is unknown to us is the path we choose because there are an infinite number of ways for us to live our lives. Relax into it. Be. Stop trying to get there and just accept that we already are. There is no place we are trying to get to. When we finally decide this is who we are, we instantly end up becoming that. This is the final stage of manifestation in becoming that which we now see ourselves as. Many people have a difficult time accepting this identity of themselves. They are still living in the illusion that they are their ego, living as a separate self, endlessly looking for a future self that does not exist.

Being authentic allows us to live in Love instead of fear. We must love ourselves enough to want to be good to ourselves. If we're not treating ourselves right and wanting what is best for us, we'll end up listening to what is a lie. That is what the ego does, creating falsehoods in what is our truth. The goal is then to move to become authentic, living as we were in Source, knowing exactly who we are, where "we're creating God through the process of being God, as we are choosing to create it," as Neale Donald Walsch says. How can we truly love ourselves when all we show to the world and ourselves is our ego?

> *"The more vulnerable we are,*
> *the stronger we become."*

Opening ourselves up and being willing to show who we are creates a situation where there are fewer things people can attack us for because we care less about how people perceive us. So, in a sense, we gain personal power. Figure out what living honestly and authentically means for you, but make sure you put aside your ego first. Otherwise, you'll be fooled by the falsehoods from your past. In this world of illusion, it's best to always choose the opposite of illusion – which is the genuineness of authenticity that is essentially us expressing God the Source in physical form.

You'll notice that many are drawn to successful people, but they become endearing to us when we see them as vulnerable as us. They become relatable, having gone through similar challenges in their life or even worse. When we embrace vulnerability, we end up being admired for being real, and for our ability to overcome it, rather than hiding behind our history of failure.

Most of us know only one way of trying to protect ourselves - by hiding our true selves and our mistakes, which is bad for our self-esteem. The problem is, there's always that one bully who's also been injured by their past, who feels they should treat us worse if only to make them feel better about themselves. So be vulnerable and most certainly, honest with yourself. Realize the wonderful world of contrast which includes bullies, that helps us to express our real untouchable selves. The whole idea of telling your truth and living in authenticity is that it's meant to help someone else. This is what sets us apart from being mediocre - to be great. The ability to touch people through our honest and authentic selves. Everything else is merely an illusion.

Finally, being authentic is not only about admitting our "mistakes," but rather it's about enjoying the rich experiential pleasure we came to this place to experience. Authenticity is about being honest as to what brings us joy in helping others through their own transformational process. And of course, as we have heard before, it's the journey that's important, not the destination. Our greatest challenges in life are our greatest successes provided we learn and grow from them. Choosing to be honest and authentic. That's what real Love is all about.

CHAPTER TEN QUESTIONS

Take a few minutes to consider each question before answering in your journal. Write as much as you're inspired to. Review later after reading the entire book to see if your answers have changed in any significant way.

- Would you say you choose how you live your life out of Love or out of the ego? How is that working for you?
- What difficult challenges from your past do you see playing a significant role in your life today?
- What things can you do today to place yourself on the path of being more honest with yourself as to how you want to live your life, free from the opinions of others?
- Explain the meaning behind this question. How can we truly love ourselves when all we show to the world and ourselves is our ego?

CHAPTER ELEVEN
JOY, HAPPINESS AND BLISS

One of the most fundamentally important things that we forget when we arrive here from Source, is to have fun while we're here on this imaginary-stage. I've suggested this as one of the two questions that will be asked of us upon our return to Spirit. How will you answer? Will you say you tried to live in joy, but life just got in the way? Was the pursuit of joy and happiness just not a priority because the focus was on trying to make enough money to keep up with the mortgage payments? Or was it that you thought joy and happiness were things that just came to us naturally and not something to work toward? It is true that before we came here, those emotions were part of our inherent existence, just like Unconditional Love. In this physical realm though, happiness arises out of choice and being aware of those brief moments of excitement. Frankly, until we experience a daily dose of joy and happiness in our lives or are fully living the bliss of sharing our gift, it's difficult to say that we're living in abundance. I still find that a challenge sometimes.

The quickest way to bring joy and happiness into our lives is by making someone else happy. The wisest way is by doing what we came here to express by following our passion and calling, devoting our lives to helping others succeed so happiness now becomes bliss and part of our everyday life.

It is through that discovery of figuring out what we are truly passionate about, that bliss reveals itself. Some of us, though we think we know what we want in life, only experience fleeting moments of the excitement that comes out of living this way. Let us make it a goal to do a little bit more each day to bring that exhilaration into our lives.

Joseph Campbell, in The Hero's Journey, also made famous the quote about following your bliss. Seeking one's identity and true calling - the Who We Are and desire to express during this lifetime.

> *"Follow your bliss*
> *and the universe will open doors*
> *where there were only walls."*
> —Joseph Campbell

Campbell describes bliss in terms of "eternal joy," and "refreshment of life all the time." During his tenure at Sarah Lawrence College as a Professor of Literature, he would sometimes see his students visibly change character when they hit upon a topic that they were excited about during their regular meetings. Their eyes would widen and their whole disposition would change as if they could see a whole new avenue of their life open up. So despite bliss being connected to happiness, the distinction for our definition is that bliss has to do your true calling. Have you ever experienced the same? It is critical to notice these fleeting moments and then follow through.

In his interview with Bill Moyers in the wonderful PBS Power of Myth series, Campbell goes on to say that bliss is a deep sense of knowing the path where our body and soul want to go, and when we discover bliss, we should hold onto it and don't let other people discourage us in following it. Nobody can tell us exactly where we're headed, nor what our bliss is, but rather than wait for it, it's something to reach for when we recognize it. When we do follow our bliss, Campbell describes it as, "like being helped by helping hands," and where, "you put yourself on sort of a track, that has been there all the while waiting for you." He also says we'll start to meet people in this same field who'll help open doors for us in the pursuit of this particular endeavor, so don't be afraid. I know this to be true for myself.

Campbell also points out the importance of moving past the feeling that we're required to do certain things in our lives, especially for younger people. He's seen so many students light up with their passion, that he encourages all of them to follow their bliss once they find it. Using the metaphor of a student studying art, one learns all the basics and rules of creating art, but at some point, they must express their own creative and individualized style.

Experts on how to become happy speak about practicing gratitude, giving compliments, performing acts of kindness, and working towards meaningful goals. These ways to become happy and find our bliss are all the things that are important to an authentic and purpose-driven life. Like Campbell says, "It is taking that pathway to purposeful engagement in life, that we're able to discover that place of true happiness and bliss. That is because it arises out of being connected to something greater than ourselves." It allows happiness, joy, and bliss to flow from deeper feelings of peace and Love and not from external measures of the ego, like how much we have or how popular we are. Like Love, where the goal is to become Love, bliss is the same, where we make the shift until it becomes an intrinsic part of Who We Are now. We come to know this to be true about ourselves when it embodies us and we feel it, living every day in the present moment with no expectations of the future because we are already what we desire. Just like in the process of manifestation, we must decide to be what we desire and then act that way before it comes to us. In this case, we decide to be this person we wish to be and then do the things that type of person does.

Another way of looking at bliss is the idea of finding meaning in our lives in the pursuit of happiness. Like Love, most of us look for meaning outside of us rather than inside. We will never discover true happiness outside of us and if we do, it will be fleeting, because it is all based on relying on others to make us feel happy and provide us with validation. Furthermore, it is not up to anyone to tell us of the deep meaning we are seeking to discover - we must find that for ourselves. Author Viktor Frankl's book, Man's Search for Meaning, believes that meaning is not something we create, but rather what we find through our circumstances. Indeed, life is a series of contrasting experiences where we choose what to believe and thus, how to ultimately find meaning for ourselves.

If you recall, I characterized our life here like a stage play where only the theme "to experience and express love" had been defined. I went on to say that we all have our scripts that are written on a moment-to-moment basis as we live our lives. This script is essentially a documentation of our search for meaning and purpose. It is through that which we are led to discover our true bliss and by extension, real happiness and joy.

Another important ingredient is Flow. I first encountered this when reading the ground-breaking book, Flow: The Psychology of Optimal Experience, by Mihaly Csikszentmihalyi. His description of the state of flow is when a person is fully connected to some activity, it allows happiness to surface. Soon after, bliss emerges after the opening of this pathway. He too, went on to say that happiness comes from

ABUNDANT SOUL ABUNDANT LIFE

inside of us, not externally. Time and time again, we see the same writing on the wall of "going inward for answers and for the things we desire," all through the meaningfulness of Love. It is all part of our permanent connection to the God Source.

Csikszentmihalyi further stated that happiness requires us to exert a certain amount of effort to bring it into our lives. No surprise. This is where we're fully engaged in what we're doing, allowing us to experience a high level of happiness without effort. It's always good to remind ourselves that some physical effort is a part of the manifestation process. Joy and happiness are not part of this individualized being that we are, so it's something important to work toward bringing it into our reality. While all of it is inherent to our original being, separation from these important emotions is the gift we're presented with. It allows us to understand and appreciate their importance as we maneuver through life as this imaginary character.

Csikszentmihalyi was born in Europe and experienced World War II during his childhood. He noticed how few adults were able to deal with the tragedies they experienced in not just losing their families, but also their homes or jobs. These significant losses made them unable to continue a normal life. This made him wonder what made a life worth living. Influenced by Carl Jung's writings, he took an interest in psychology, later moving to America, and began to seek answers about the roots of happiness.

Scientists have determined our brain is in the alpha wave state while in *flow*, which correlates to inspirational thought or the connection to our higher self. This is where beautiful music and art are created and insights into things not yet imagined on earth are being manifested. It is when we connect to the God Source that there is an unlimited supply of Love, joy, and happiness built into our DNA. But it won't come to us automatically as it normally does in Spirit. No, we must work for it here. Joy, happiness, and bliss are vibrational emotions available to us at any time and in unlimited quantities, once we step into the state of Being Love and Being Joy and fully embrace that which we are.

Surveys taken of Americans from the mid-1950s for four decades measured their level of happiness with their income. During those forty years, a person's happiness remained relatively constant at around 30%, plus or minus a few points, while income more than doubled. This showed that happiness has little to do with how much money we make. The conclusion was that after a person's basic needs were met, the bigger house or fancier car wouldn't bring meaningful and sustained happiness.

Csikszentmihalyi identified nine characteristics we experience to let us know we are in the state of Flow:

1. Our skills in doing the activity pretty much match that of how challenging it is.
2. When we're fully engaged and seriously focused on the task at hand, or where "action and awareness" are merged.
3. Where we know what our purpose is and have a clear picture of each step we are to take along the way.
4. Where we're getting immediate and clear feedback as to our progress.
5. While we're extremely focused on the task at hand, we are oblivious to all internal and external distractions.
6. Feeling like we are in full control of the situation without any worry of failing.
7. The loss of self-consciousness or where we have little concern about what others might think of us while doing this activity.

8. Where we lose track of time because we're so deeply engaged in the activity.
9. Just doing and experiencing the activity is the reward in itself.

Csikszentmihalyi notes a combination of the first three starts the Flow experience process and that each one standing by itself does not constitute being in the Flow. Let's take a closer look into each of them.

In the first characteristic, Csikszentmihalyi sees this where our skill level pretty much matches the challenge at hand. Too easy and simple, we get bored. Too difficult, we end up being frustrated and quit. We get into the Flow experience by maintaining this balance that ultimately moves us to a higher level of enjoyment as we reach new levels. As we acquire more experience and skill, the activity should also have the ability to ramp up accordingly. One of the best examples of this is some video games that continually challenge us with new levels of difficulty - once we conquer the preceding ones.

The second characteristic is a situation where all our attention is completely focused on what we're doing. All our concerns or worries we've had before getting into this state disappear. I'm sure we've all been there before where we found ourselves so engrossed in the task at hand, without a care in the world.

The third characteristic is that we have a clear picture of what we desire and what the outcome will look like. We know what to do next and every step thereafter. There is no ambiguity, unlike normally where there are so many things that deserve our attention that things become cloudy.

The fourth characteristic is when we receive immediate feedback on our progress as we are doing the activity, so we can make the necessary changes to keep us in the Flow state. When I think of this, it reminds me of a Motocross competition where the rider knows the course well. With each turn, dip, and hill, the rider is continually getting feedback on how well they're handling their bike through the handlebars and the motorcycle itself. They can feel how they are doing, allowing them to make split-second decisions on exactly when to accelerate during the next turn or prepare for the next hill coming up until they reach the finish line.

The fifth characteristic is when we're doing something, fully connected, and engaged in the activity without any distractions. I remember when I was a kid, I loved building model airplanes. It was almost like I was in a dream state as I looked at the instructions, found the correct pieces, then glued the tiny pieces together to make the engine and the body, being careful I was doing it right. And slowly but surely, I'd see it materialize before my eyes. Then add some different colored paint where indicated and apply some decals to the body and wings. In the end, I had completed a beautiful 3D model of the photo on the box that I kept on my shelf until it got so dusty that my mom threw it away. Sometimes my friends would want me to come outside and play, but nothing could pull me away from finishing.

Sixth, Csikszentmihalyi labels this as having a total feeling of control, where failure is not part of the equation. I like to describe this as feeling "invincible" because our confidence is heightened in the process of "doing" this activity. It is not about second-guessing ourselves.

As the seventh characteristic, this is where we're "in the zone," totally engaged in our activity with little worry about how others see and perceive us. Self-consciousness becomes a non-issue because we're too focused on what we're doing to care. This is where the ego disappears to reveal our real self to others. For many people who know how to dance well enough, this is a prime example of this characteristic. Gliding out there on the dance floor, cha-cha cha-ing, square dancing, or doing the waltz, where they're having fun on the dance floor. Unlike some of us, me included, who are silently counting, "1 left foot, 2 right foot, 1 left foot..." in our heads, and making sure we don't step on the toes of our dance partner. I'm pretty sure that's not in the Flow.

The eighth characteristic of being in Flow is when we lose all track of time because our attention is so sharply focused on the given activity that we're engaged in. I think of examples where an acquaintance stops us on the street and asks us about a particular topic we're extremely passionate about. We end up talking for a long time and yet it feels like only a few minutes have passed. This happened to me while I was interviewing Steve Allen, where they gave me 45 minutes for the session, but we chatted for over two and a half hours. We both had lost all sense of time as our conversation continued on and on.

Lastly, the ninth characteristic is when the activity itself becomes its reward or autotelic. This is the idea of doing something just for the enjoyment it brings -

for the pure sake of doing it, and for the experience, nothing else. Here again, what we get out of this originates from within us rather than outside. A good example is any form of art like painting or sculpting. I've seen some people meticulously paint for hours, so engrossed in their creation.

Beyond Flow, there's the practice of gratitude, which we now know is extremely important. Experiencing and expressing gratitude is key to making others feel good about themselves and worthy enough to be loved, not only by others but more importantly by themselves. Remember, the quickest way to become happy is to help someone else in their life. To create a sustainable way of being happy all the time for ourselves, it logically follows that we should make our main goal to help others find happiness too. We get there by following our own bliss to find purpose and meaning in our lives.

Remember to be a little kinder to ourselves because all the lies we believed in the past no longer serve us, except to provide a contextual experience of the opposite of what we are seeking. Love yourself. It's the first step to opening yourself to the wisdom that's inside you.

Another factor important in happiness is the creation of strong social connections with others. Find a community that speaks the same "language," where they support your dreams and desires, and where you feel good being around them. Sincerely compliment others everywhere you go, and in your support community, create a time when you complement each other for meaningful things and not superficial things like, "Oh, your hair looks nice today." Have deep conversations occasionally with your friends and be more expressive and authentic in who you are. We may have been born into this world alone, but it's through others that we enjoy it.

Relax and don't take things so seriously as life is supposed to be about Love and having fun. See this place for what it is, a playground where you're having fun. Like the first time you went on the slide, sometimes things are uncomfortable until you do it. Exchange jokes that don't offend anyone. Be intentional in remembering and cherishing all the great things we've experienced and the simple pleasures we enjoy in our lives.

And of course, get and stay healthy, exercise, go outside in nature and enjoy the sun, meditate, and be good to yourself. Choose positive vibrational energies rather than lower negative ones. Make laughing out loud a habit and create situations where that happens often. After morning gratitude exercises, put on some upbeat music that raises your mood and empowers you. Finally, remind yourself of how worthy you are and what contributions and special gifts you bring to the world. Remembering that will see you through many stressful situations.

CHAPTER ELEVEN QUESTIONS

Take a few minutes to consider each question before answering in your journal. Write as much as you're inspired to. Review later after reading the entire book to see if your answers have changed in any significant way.

- Where do you see happiness arising from; other people or from inside us? Explain your reasoning.
- Describe in detail how happy you would be if you were living the life you wanted for yourself right now. Take as much time on this and have fun and be as descriptive as possible. Use this to help fashion your True Self of Being you wish to manifest for yourself.
- What are some examples from your own life that confirm that you have been in Flow at one time or another?
- How many of the nine characteristics of Flow can you identify with that you have experienced?

CHAPTER TWELVE
THE ART OF LIVING YOU

Truth be told, to make the final leap to heal one's abundance and awaken to that state is not an easy one. It requires us to open ourselves to see beyond the veil of what we believe is physically real. To move past the ego of self and see us through the eyes of God. This is what the "art of living you" is, to be honest with ourselves and express who we really are rather than what we think others want us to be. This is stepping into a higher level of vibratory understanding where the purpose of our experience here is not about "getting," but rather "giving." It's meant to break through notions of individuality, good vs. evil and most of all, fear and uncertainty.

Embracing the Love that is our true identity, leads us to only one conclusion as to why we are even here. It's about discovering our true calling on what brings us the most joy, to find as many people as possible to share that with and have a lot of fun doing it. When you can come to that place in your life, you have mastered the art of living you.

A memorable life is often created
by leaping into the unknown
that our heart is whispering for us to follow.

Let us review and recap the major points to take away that have been discussed here:

- We all come from the God Source or Spirit to this physical playground or stage play, to help expand the Universe, despite its imaginary façade.
- The fullness of our lives comes by way of exploring, making mistakes, creating what we desire, and having as much fun as possible.
- Coming from a place where we are all One and a part of God, into a world of delusional

separation, we experience different stages of development.
- We heal abundantly when we get to a space where we feel worthy enough to be loved. The goal is to share that love with others to help them find their way, therefore, worthiness is a necessary component to healing our abundance.
- The main theme is to experience and express Love in its fullest way, yet we decide the pathway to take, and how we want to express that Love.
- The ultimate expression of Love, of course, is how we choose to live our lives, one driven by passion and authenticity, another by fear.
- Love and happiness are not feelings to be sought from other people or outside of us, but rather inward and through our connection to the Spirit.
- It is the presence of Love that allows us to see our "enemies," as:

--helping to strengthen us
--to give us more courage
--to assist us in valuing ourselves more

--to help us understand compassion and
--to connect with the Love that always exists within all of us.

- Everything is made up of vibrational energy, so nothing ever "dies" except to change its form of vibrational frequency.
- When we understand that all of our negative emotions allow us to experience a contrasting emotional vibration, it is through that experience that we can move into becoming stronger, and more courageous, having more gratitude for other people and our lives here, and a host of other empowering things.
- Through the law of opposites, we're presented with contrast in our lives to help us decide how we wish to act and express ourselves as who we wish to be.
- Our greatest fears help us figure out what are passions are.
- The idea is to see our differences as something to value as the gift that I give to others, ultimately becomes the gift that is given to myself.

- Every single person we come in contact with in some form or another, helps to shape our view of things or how we act.
- Contrast is important in understanding the illusion of separation here in this world, as is death and loss.
- Death and loss are merely illusions meant to create a contextual field for our temporary existence here and is an unbroken circle of birth and death, birth, and death.
- In death, when we're able to emerge from the so-called darkness of sorrow and onto the other side of reasoning, we open ourselves up to profound changes in what the meaning of life is, and in discovering what our deepest passion is and what we came here to do. Loss is fundamental to our physical human development in that sometimes we must lose something or rid ourselves of it, to make space for something new to come into our lives.
- This separated identity known as the "ego" is to see others and ourselves to decide how we want to act and appear to one another and how we fit in.

- The ego convinces us that the true love we yearn to experience and express does not exist or is extremely rare, when in fact it is impossible to disconnect from the God Source of Unconditional Love.
- Initially, the ego helps us to define our identity, however, the challenge is to move beyond that to becoming authentic and living with purpose.
- It is the ego that sets us off on a path of discovering untruths because the answers don't lie outside of us, but rather inside.
- The ego always measures our self-worth as to how we're doing compared with someone else. Competition is the key word here.
- Finding your bliss or passion in life provides meaning, which enables us to experience Love and happiness in our lives.
- The Vision Quest or Hero's Journey is a process of discovering and remembering who we are so we can step into BEING.
- Not everyone will choose this path and not every soul will make the journey, but for those that do make the journey and succeed, our eyes open to our bliss or what we wish to accomplish.

- Authenticity is our natural state of being as God while in this physical realm.
- By deciding to move from using our ego to one of authenticity, we give up the unnecessary struggle.
- Authenticity means to be open and willing to be vulnerable, knowing that others in the world are here to challenge us and help us, all from the perspective of Love.
- Living authentically and being honest with ourselves, helps us discover our purpose and true bliss, and opens us to receiving and expressing gratitude.
- Most people do not fully embrace forgiveness, but gratitude enables us to see all of our past, both good and bad, as being beneficial to our experience here.
- Gratitude also helps us to feel worthy of being loved and to the abundance we seek.
- Both gratitude and Love are two feelings that are crucial if we wish to manifest anything positive in our lives.
- The basis of the Law of Attraction, which has its roots in quantum physics, is where our negative or positive feelings about something, align us with people, things, and

- situations whether good or bad of similar vibrational rates of energy.
- Whereas the Law of Assumption, also rooted in quantum physics, starts with the notion that one has already arrived, so how we feel is important.
- The manifestation process is the act of continually focusing our thoughts, emotions, and feelings on what we desire in our lives in a very real way it produces a change in our identity.
- We bring to us that which we are, not what we want.
- One of the most challenging things in the manifestation process is taking the step into "being." The illusion of time makes it difficult to imagine just stepping into a future reality. Except that it is not a future persona of ourselves, but rather just another vibrational version of us. The True Being of Self.
- Like everything else, procrastination and self-sabotage can both hinder or help our progress.
- Time is an illusion of the ego to keep us believing in the separation of ourselves. It

implies a certain distance left to go before something will manifest for us.
- Wanting and needing do not bring us what we desire in manifestation because they imply lack.
- Form a "crowd creation" group to help bring these other vibrational versions of ourselves into reality. Relax and surrender as that obstruction you may be trying to get through could be only three feet wide, easy enough to walk around.
- Most of us believe money/wealth is like a pie where there are only so many pieces to go around when in reality, money is pure vibration, so in no way are there limits on its availability.
- We've developed so much fear and anxiety around money because we don't understand it and feel it controls our entire lives.
- Work towards befriending your money, rather than having it be a stranger to us.
- The extent of how much we deserve in life is directly influenced by how much we love ourselves.
- The quickest way to bring joy and happiness into our lives is by making

someone else happy, but the wisest way is by following our passion and helping others. So, happiness now becomes a part of our everyday life.

- "Follow your bliss and the universe will open doors where there were only walls." - Joseph Campbell
- Every single tear you cry today becomes another joy and happy memory in the end - if you're willing to understand the purpose of this pathway to discovery that we're all on.
- The human journey of the soul's desire for fulfillment begins when we discover what we love to do in life and have the desire to share that deep Love with others.

The road to realizing that abundance has been sitting right next to us all this time is not just simply reciting a bunch of mantras. Rather, it's about taking a deeper look into our past hurts and challenges, which are often shrouded in darkness. This search of our past allows us to shine a light upon those things to help us find clarity and peace.

We must come to understand that every difficult and traumatic experience we've had to endure (growing up and in our later years), originates from the place of Unconditional Love. Everything. The underlying answer to manifesting anything is to the extent of how much we love ourselves. No situation or person does not come from this place because, in Source, Love is all there is - it is the beginning and the ending.

This includes all of the different people involved in our lives from our parents, siblings, enemies, and even the drunk driver that caused deep emotional wounds and sadness to occur. This may be a very difficult concept to accept, but without that understanding, healing could take a very long time or for that matter, may never happen, at least not during this lifetime. It is a difficult paradigm to transcend for many to go from hate and guilt to one of Love and gratitude. Whatever the case, the journey is still worth it.

*"Our hunger to find ways of experiencing
and expressing Love into the world
is satisfied through the hardships we encounter.
So rejoice your hard times,
as they won't last forever."*

We stop seeing everything and everybody outside of us as the cause of our pain and happiness and answer to our problems. Love doesn't originate from others; it must begin with us internally. In reaching this place, we're no longer dependent on our partner, family, or friends to Love us and make us feel worthy. Once we reach this place for ourselves, our relationship with others has the potential to become a much healthier, mutually supportive type of Love to share.

Our movement to where everything emanates from inside of us means being connected to the Source God and connected to the power we've always possessed.

When ready, we step into that identity of our true self where we discover the place that Love, and happiness originates. This is the "Art of Living You," where forgiveness becomes irrelevant and is replaced by gratitude that emerges from our hearts. The more gratitude we experience, the more we feel worthy of being Loved and the more we feel Loved, the more we open ourselves up to receiving complete abundance and being healed where struggle is but a faint memory.

At that point, abundance has arrived at our doorstep, and has asked to come in. It's time to open the door and let it in.

CHAPTER TWELVE QUESTIONS

It should be no surprise for you to hear at this point when I say that everything starts and ends with Love. The essence of achieving true abundance is making the decision to live this bold and courageous version of yourself. I'm assuming since you've come this far, you've already made that decision.

You're about to embark on your own hero's journey and to be open to a new way of seeing things and expressing yourself to support others. But the one thing we must embody before anything else is self-love. Unless we love ourselves enough to bring what we want into our lives to materialize, we may never reach this goal.

For the next 14-30 days, make a list of experiences in your life that you're extremely proud of accomplishing. It could be an achievement of yours or a major challenge you've overcome such as being homeless to now owning you own home. Don't rush on this as it's extremely important. Next, take each one and write in here or in your journal "I love you because (your accomplishment)." Some examples are:

- *I love you because you never gave up when times were extremely tough.*
- *I love you because of your willingness to be vulnerable and real.*
- *I love you because you're willing to be open to new ways of looking at things.*
- *I love you because of your commitment to living your best life and to be a living example of that.*

Throughout the day, reread each of these statements preferably while looking at yourself in the mirror. Whether you do or not, what's most important is that you feel the positive loving energy being expressed. If looking in the mirror is not your thing, share your take-aways in your journal. The more you internalize these statements, the more expansive your ability to accept your new identity. Just make sure these accomplishments bring a sense of pride and self-esteem to your soul.

If you feel some apprehension in anything you write, see if this feeling arises from a past wound that still needs healing. This may manifest as some sort of sabotage or procrastination in what we want to. Have a conversation with your real self in your journal to see if any fears are associated with this cleansing. What are your concerns? Then open yourself up to see what it's telling you. Just don't judge the message. Chances are, you'll discover you were wrong about all those fears you've created in your mind. Life is waiting to unfold that'll be even better than you could've ever imagined.

Take all the time you need as loving ourselves is integral in the process of changing our identity. Recall that our ability to accept more abundance is directly connected to our worthiness. If you need more time, so be it. Until you've dealt with you hidden wounds, moving into a new identity for yourself will be difficult, if not extremely challenging to manifest.

When ready, sharpen up your description of this new identity of yours. Daydream in "high definition" of what this image will be along with what you'll be thinking about on a day-to-day basis, how you'll be feeling, what you'll be wearing and what you'll do when you get up first thing in the morning. Spend a week if necessary.

Describe what the greatest expression of who you wish to be during this lifetime that brings you the most joy and happiness.

When finished, at the bottom, make a firm commitment to stepping into this new persona within the timeframe chosen. Then sign and date it.

I commit to fully becoming this new identity within one year (or whatever timeframe you choose) from today.
Signed:
Date:

Be sure to choose a reasonable deadline but something that still feels a little uncomfortable. Then put your commitment where you can see it every day. If you fail to make that date, check to see if there are still some blocks in the way. Keep working at it.

> *"The journey to what we seek only feels long because we're not enjoying the trip. Once we do, we end up complaining at how short it was."*

EPILOGUE

There's one thing I hope you'll take away from this book that I've been incessantly talking about from the beginning and now at the end. Need I repeat myself? It is to recognize how important Love is while on our journey here. The power we all possess inside ourselves is only limited by how we feel about ourselves. So find it in you and then help someone else find for themselves. All that is required is for you to express you to bring the abundance you seek. Despite what many would think in this segregated world, we are all working together in a grand symphony. Even "Us against them" also has as its origins in pure unconditional love.

Truth be told, I never thought this book would turn out to be about the subject of Love. But the more I allowed inspired thought to come to me, the more I realized I needed to share this with others like yourself. Maybe instead of hurting each other we look inward and find the Love we deserve for ourselves.

> *"I'm not living this life to impress anyone*
> *with my accomplishments*
> *nor with climbing the highest mountain.*
> *I'm just here to be Love*
> *and to help one other person*
> *feel the same for themselves."*

It'll never be a perfect world from our limited view, for what exactly is perfection? How else could we experience and express ourselves unless we had contrast in it? Duality is important to help us to believe in the separateness of this illusional place.

My last piece of advice is to forget about the critics, especially the one most critical living inside of us. Speak your truth, sing your song and paint that masterpiece that is uniquely you. Create a life you Love that Loves you with amazing vibrant colors and incredible hues. This is the authentic Art of Living You.

SPECIAL MESSAGE FROM THE AUTHOR

Hi everyone, if you're reading this, then most likely you've read the entire book. I really hope it's helping you start to change the way you look at things that'll allow you to understand what your purpose is and also give you practical tools to bring true abundance into your life filled with Love, happiness and wealth.

While I was extremely delighted to have received such glowing endorsements from my mentors, who I now call my friends, such as Neale Donald Walsch of the *Conversations with God* Series, long time author Alan Cohen on his many, many books including *The Course in Miracles Made Easy* and his award winning book *A Deep Breath of Life*, and the Zen Master Author himself, Ken Honda who's critically acclaimed books, *Happy Money* and *True Wealth*, have helped millions learn about money, it is you the reader that I wrote this book for.

If you've enjoyed it and have found it useful, please do me a favor and leave an honest review on Amazon and any other review sites you can think of. I know this book won't resonate with everybody as some may not be in the right place to hear the message as yet, but the only way that could ever happen is to make them aware of this book. So as a personal request from me to you, please reach out to any of your friends, family and soulful communities you're a part of to share this message of Love with them. Perhaps it'll help others to discover the passion inside themselves to take the first step. Or maybe its message of Love could help them get over a difficult time in their life, so they're able to see you at the end of their darkness holding a candle to light the way out for them. Whatever the case, this is our purpose. To help others find their way to loving themselves more and allow abundance to flow into their lives that we all rightly deserve.

Please also make sure you register on my website using the link or QR code below to learn about my new books, special offers made only to special subscribers like yourself, scheduled appearances I'll be doing at various amazing and inspiring events and my private consultations and amazing courses and retreats being planned.

www.gharydavidwon.com

I may have written this book with the help from my angels and spirit guides, but I need your help to spread the importance of Love in everything we do. I believe this book is meant to be for the many, many of you needing to find your way to true abundance.

Love and blessings,
Ghary David Won

THERE'S ALSO A COMPANION WORKBOOK AVAILABLE!

Embark on an immersive journey of self-discovery and empowerment with the companion workbook to *Abundant Soul, Abundant Life*. Dive deeper into the book's wisdom with insightful exercises and reflections that amplify your understanding and application of gratitude-based principles. Enhance your quest of abundance and fulfillment with this illuminating companion tailored for those hungry for lasting transformation.

The companion Abundant Soul, Abundant Life Workbook available in ebook and audiobook formats

Available only as an eBook or audiobook.

Purchase online at Amazon, various other retailers or directly on my website (register for special offers).

ebook ISBN 9798991096454
audiobook ISBN 9798991096478

BIBLIOGRAPHY

- Arigato Living Community, http://www.kenhonda.com, 2021
- Blackham, Dr. Kim, The Three Levels of Gratitude: Understanding how Gratitude Changes Lives, Article http://www.kimblackham.com
- Campbell, Joseph, Assorted works including The Hero with a Thousand Faces, Pantheon Books 1949
- Csikszentmihalyi, Mihaly, Flow: The Psychology of Optimal Experience, Harper & Row 1990, 303p
- Dyer, Wayne, Real Magic: Creating Miracles in Everyday Life, HarperCollins 1992, 270p, and other assorted works
- Viktor Frankl, Man's Search for Meaning, Verlag für Jugend und Volk, 1946 (Austria), Beacon Press 1959 (English), 200p
- Honda, Ken, Happy Money: The Japanese Art of Making Peace with Your Money, Gallery Books 2019, 240p
- McCrum, Sarah, Love Money, Money Loves You: A Conversation with the Energy of Money, Sarah McCrum 2022, 286p
- PBS, Joseph Campbell and the Power of Myth, Staring Bill Moyers and Joseph Campbell, 1988, 360 minutes
- Schucman, Helen, A Course in Miracles, Viking: The Foundation for Inner Peace 1976, 1333p
- Walsch, Neale Donald, Conversations with God, Book 1, Hampton Roads 1995, 216p, and other assorted works

Other mentions:

- Gesell, Silvio, Expiring Money
- Houston, Jean, https://www.jeanhouston.com
- IANDS, International Association of Near-Death Studies
- Schwinger effect, Dr. Julian Schwinger
- Suits, American Television Series, 2011-19, Produced by Universal Content Productions
- Wörgl , Austrian town

ABOUT THE AUTHOR

Ghary David Won, a dedicated explorer of the human spiritual saga, has navigated diverse and less-traveled paths, laden with unexpected turns. Leaving behind a lengthy corporate career post-education, he chose an unconventional path, abandoning conventional confines for a life enriched with unique experiences that grant him a distinctive outlook on our authentic purpose and how to leverage it for embracing the abundance we all deserve. Ghary immersed himself in the profound realms of hospice care, mortality, and a ten-month bout of homelessness, living in a car, to gain unparalleled insights into life's depths.

Through his groundbreaking book, Abundant Soul, Abundant Life: The Art of Living You, Ghary shares practical strategies rooted in love's transformative strength to guide individuals towards a genuinely abundant and purposeful existence that he has personally discovered.